"Give me one hundred preachers who fear

nothing but sin, and desire nothing but God, and

I care not a straw whether they be clergymen or

laymen; such alone will shake the gates of hell and

set up the kingdom of heaven on Earth."

John Wesley

IMPACT!

Reclaiming the Call of Lay Ministry

by Kay Kotan and Blake Bradford

Market
Square
BOOKS

IMPACT!
Reclaiming the Call of Lay Ministry

©2018 Market Square Publishing Company, LLC.
books@marketsquarebooks.com
P.O. Box 23664 Knoxville, Tennessee 37933

ISBN: 978-0-9987546-9-7

Library of Congress: 2018940702

Printed and Bound in the United States of America

Cover Illustration & Book Design ©2018 Market Square Publishing, LLC
Cover Design by Kevin Slimp
Page Layout by Earl Goodman
Editor: Kevin Slimp

Table of Contents

——————— IMPACT! ———————

Introduction

Meet the Authors

Kay Kotan

Kay is a passionate layperson who happens to be a fourth-generation Methodist. She has taken the normal windy-turny road on her faith journey – sometimes being far from God while other times being best buds. She is a wife to Bob and mother to an adult son, Cameron.

Kay has served in a variety of leadership roles in the local church and has most recently been a part of a movement for church transformation nationally. She is a credentialed, professional coach as well as a consultant and author of more than a dozen church leadership books.

Her current ministry setting includes serving as the Director of Congregational Development for the Susquehanna Conference of the United Methodist Church. She was not only called by God to move halfway across the country from Missouri to Pennsylvania to serve God, but she has been called to help the laity reclaim their Wesleyan roots of lay church leadership.

Blake Bradford

Blake is an ordained elder (presbyter) in the United Methodist Church. While he did not grow up attending church regularly as a child, he found a warm welcome when he began driving his grandmother to worship at her beloved United Methodist congregation in Little Rock. He attended a church-affiliated college (Hendrix College in Conway, Arkansas) and began taking theology and church history classes. He discovered a great joy in learning about God and the people of God through the centuries, so he went to Vanderbilt University for a Master of Arts degree in Medieval and Reformation Theology.

Along the way, God started working, and he joined the United Methodist Church, eventually hearing and responding to a call to attend seminary and to seek ordination. Never one to stop learning, Blake also studied at SMU's Perkins School of Theology and earned the Doctor of Ministry degree.

Blake has served in churches of different sizes and contexts in Colorado and Arkansas as an associate pastor, solo pastor of a small church in a county seat, and senior pastor of a mid-sized congregation in the city. His most recent parish appointment has been as executive pastor of a 3500-member congregation where he worked with clergy, staff, and lay leadership to align and coordinate the church's ministries.

Blake has spent much of his time in ministry focused on the leadership of the clergy: He served on the executive committee of the Arkansas Conference Board of Ordained Ministry for several years, created and directed their Residency In Ministry Program for those seeking ordination, and taught pastoral leadership and administration for the Arkansas Course of Study School. Blake was appointed to the Arkansas Conference's Center for Vitality, resourcing and coaching congregations to make an impact in their communities. He is currently serving as the District Superintendent and Chief Mission Strategist for the Central District of the Arkansas Annual Conference. It is through his ministry working alongside intentional lay-clergy teams that Blake has felt called to address the amazing and often untapped potential impact of lay leadership.

Why Blake and Kay Together?

Our (Blake and Kay's) ministry paths collided a few years back. We have come to respect our unique pathways in ministry as clergy and laity. In our collaborative work together, we discovered we both highly value and encourage lay leadership and lay/clergy ministry synergy. We have also discovered the widespread devaluation of lay leadership by both the laity and clergy and the under-functioning of lay leadership. If we are to once again become a movement to reach new people, we must once again be about the potential IMPACT of lay leadership. Because of our passions in empowering the laity, we felt compelled to offer some insights, equipping, and encouragement for the laity. We feel our unique lens of both a clergy and a laity viewpoint – both collectively and individually – might be helpful for all. Our prayer is, this resource will encourage the laity to IMPACT their mission fields for Christ.

Why IMPACT?

We, the authors (Blake and Kay), believe in the power of laity in the local churches. The church likely rises and falls with the missional investment of the laity. So, of course, this book is for the laity, but it is also for pastors and judicatory leaders. Our hope for this resource is to rekindle the spark and set the laity on fire – on fire for Christ. Our tribe, the United Methodist Church, was founded as a movement of laity and reached millions of people. Our hope and prayer is that this resource will help re-engage and empower the laity. Our founder, John Wesley, began and sustained a very powerful and effective lay movement that made disciples amidst the fracturing of the Industrial age and the Enlightenment. Wesley believed all could provide IMPACT:

> **"Give me one hundred preachers who fear nothing but sin, and desire nothing but God, and I care not a straw whether they be clergymen or laymen; such alone will shake the gates of hell and set up the kingdom of heaven on Earth."** 1

We pray that lay leaders and disciples in the pews will discover encouragement and resources in these pages to lead the church in our disciple-making mission in today's complex and confusing world.

This resource is meant to challenge the reader and his/her respective church. It is also meant to help spark critical and crucial conversations to empower the laity for ministry with IMPACT! It is our core belief that a church who demon-

---

1 John Wesley, in a 1777 letter to Alexander Mather, quoted in Luke Tyerman, *The Life and Times of the Rev. John Wesley.* London, 1871. III:632. Northwest Nazarene University has created the Wesley Center Online website to be a collection of historical and scholarly resources about the Wesleyan tradition. This full letter, along with many historical documents of the Wesleyan and Methodist movement, can be found at http://wesley.nnu.edu/john-wesley/the-letters-of-john-wesley/wesleys-letters-1777.

strates ministry with IMPACT is a church that has a strong movement of the Christ-centered laity. This lay movement understands the purpose of the church and what it means to be a fully committed follower of Jesus Christ who transforms the world.

The fourth chapter of Ephesians helps us understand the call to ministry of the laity. ALL (not only clergy) are called into ministry, and ALL are gifted for ministry.[2] A key element of the Protestant Reformation was the affirmation of the priesthood of all believers. Five hundred years after Martin Luther nailed the 95 Theses to the Wittenberg Church door and affirmed the priesthood of all believers, we are still coming to terms with the consequences of the Reformation's affirmation that the laity are indeed called into ministry. This book will explore the ways in which the laity have given away their ministry or maybe, even in some cases, have found their ministry stripped away. You will also find ideas and resources for how to reclaim lay ministry and be empowered to renew the laity movement.

The historical drift towards the professionalization of congregational leadership has created an enormous challenge for us as laity. As Methodists, we have left behind our Founder's roots as a movement of laity and, instead, become a pastor-centered and pastor-dependent movement. After master's degrees were required for ordained clergy in the 1950s, the drift began in earnest. Next, larger and larger churches have been required to afford the professional clergy due to the costs associated with their compensation package. Then came the movement to describe senior pastors as CEOs

---

2 So Christ himself gave the apostles, the prophets, the evangelists, the pastors and teachers, 12 to equip his people for works of service, so that the body of Christ may be built up. (Ephesians 4:11−12, NIV).

of the churches they are serving. With each successive drift, it widened the gap between the leadership development of the laity and clergy. Each step depowered laity more and more. The clergy became the 'experts,' relying on the laity more for technical expertise (such as finances or building programs) and less on strategic matters. Today, there is a great divide between the leadership formation of the clergy and laity. I (Kay) have experienced a pervasive apathy of congregations and laity leadership, as I have consulted and coached throughout the country. I believe this apathy is at least partly to blame on the institutionalized professionalization of church leadership.

Our young people today are looking to engage their leadership in a very different method than leaders of the past. Our younger leaders desire authenticity and transparency. If we are to connect and engage with young leaders, we will have to shift our practices of church leadership. A millennial leader told me (Kay) recently that young adult leaders have a very sensitive BS meter. They value 'R & R' – being raw and real. How are we opening up spaces and leading differently in order for young leaders to desire to lead?

This is actually not a new problem. In Acts chapter 6, we read about the first church argument. In this case, the conflict was rooted in a complex matrix of people and priorities: the chosen leaders (the apostles), the relational ministry and mission of the church (the Greek-speaking widows), congregational resource allocation (the apostles' time and the distribution of food) and the larger congregation of Christ followers (the whole community of disciples). The critical question 2000 years ago was: Would the apostles continue to manage the food distribution, therefore holding back the greater mission of the church? Or would they share ministry with the larger faith community of disciples, expanding the potential IMPACT of the fledgeling church? How the apostles and the church creatively approached this problem shows their dedication to the mission that Christ gave them. The apostles were self-aware enough to focus on their role of nurturing the grace-filled Word of God. Meanwhile, the larger faith community selected the laity from among their ranks to lead the missional ministry of the church. The disciples selected seven leaders, and the apostles prayed and laid hands on these lay leaders. The next verse shares what happens when clergy stop hoarding ministry and start empowering the laity:

> **The word of God continued to spread; the number of the disciples increased greatly in Jerusalem, and a great many of the priests became obedient to the faith.**[3]

An IMPACT! Team

Both of us (Blake and Kay) have spent years working with congregational vision teams. Unfortunately, too many times the vision team spends months, or even years, working on vision statements (which often become *marketing statements* that never are used in daily decision-making). Along the way, the congregational leaders on the vision team, who have been doing A LOT of visioning, get exhausted with it all and never get around to actually changing *behaviors* to make an IMPACT on the congregation, let alone an IMPACT on the community. We highly suggest a church team journey through this resource together. Why not considering pulling together an IMPACT Team? A group of ten to twelve people is a good size to initially work through this resource. To

---

3 Acts 6:7, NIV

build your IMPACT Team, gather the pastor, a couple of key ministry leaders (which could include staff), a few current leaders, and a few younger regular attenders who you sense are looking for something more in the life of the church. By combining new and established leaders, you are creating the opportunity for mentoring and cross-mentoring. This is a chance for the established leaders to bring historical and traditional elements to the conversations and the new leaders to bring new perspectives from younger generations to the table. You might even consider adding people from the community to your group.

Allow me to share a story about the power of bringing a variety of people to the table. I (Kay) had the privilege of working with a church plant of sorts. There was a remnant group of about 35 people who decided to turn their assets (building, prime location, and a large endowment) over to an anchor church in their town for a second campus. As part of the rebuilding/restart/second campus process, the church went through a visioning process. The pastor was brilliant in how she brought the team together.

The team consisted of a couple of people from the remnant group, a few new people who were recently connected to the church, de-churched people who lived in the area, and a person deeply involved in the surrounding area's business and organizations. This team prayed together, prayer walked, studied the demographics of the area, conducted interviews with city leaders and business owners, studied books together, and reviewed examples of church vision statements.

I have yet to experience anything else like what happened within this group. Not only was there relationship building, but there was a growing great respect for one another's views, beliefs, and dreams. Together, this team not only discerned God's new vision, but they also created the much-needed excitement, enthusiasm, and momentum to do a new thing for this new day to reach new people. The unique blending of these leaders from various walks of life from the mission field created this rare opportunity to bring relevant voices to the table to discern God's preferred future for the church.

This book has three sections. The first two chapters outline the nature and mission of the church. Chapters Three through Six focus on the IMPACT potential of congregations through different lenses of ministry. The last two chapters are designed primarily for the laity with leadership responsibilities in their congregations. At the end of each chapter, you will find some questions to help spur conversations. There are questions for leaders, disciples in the pew, and pastors or staff. We encourage you to really spend some time wrestling with these questions. Shifts, clarity, and new direction will be found in your wrestling and in your honest conversation. Once you walk through this resource with the initial group, you may find the desire to start other IMPACT Teams who will not only study the materials but begin to ask new questions that will transition your congregation for even larger IMPACT. We pray this process will ignite a movement in your church for a God-sized IMPACT!

Our Hoped-for Outcomes: A God-Sized IMPACT

We are a people OF transformation and FOR transformation. We are a community of people coming together for a common purpose. That purpose is Christ-centered and

God-sized IMPACT! IMPACT will be best realized when we are a mission- and vision-guided church who is lay-governed, pastor-led, and filled with laity who are equipped and mobilized for ministry.

When we walk alongside congregations in coaching or consulting relationships, we have discovered the importance of starting with the end in mind. For us, your companions on this journey, our 'end in mind' is that the laity in your congregation would join together for a God-sized IMPACT in souls and neighborhoods, in congregations and communities, in your heart and in God's big world. Let's start our journey of IMPACT!

Chapter One

Christ's Church for Christ's Impact

Who do you think Paul is, anyway? Or Apollos, for that matter? Servants, both of us – servants who waited on you as you gradually learned to entrust your lives to our mutual Master. We each carried out our servant assignment. I planted the seed, Apollos watered the plants, but God made you grow. It's not the one who plants or the one who waters who is at the center of this process but God, who makes things grow. Planting and watering are menial servant jobs at minimum wages. What makes them worth doing is the God we are serving. You happen to be God's field in which we are working.

Or, to put it another way, you are God's house. Using the gift God gave me as a good architect, I designed blueprints; Apollos is putting up the walls. Let each carpenter who comes on the job take care to build on the foundation! Remember, there is only one foundation, the one already laid: Jesus Christ. Take particular care in picking out your building materials. Eventually there is going to be an inspection. If you use cheap or inferior materials, you'll be found out. The inspection will be thorough and rigorous. You won't get by with a thing. If your work passes inspection, fine; if it doesn't, your part of the building will be torn out and started over. But you won't be torn out; you'll survive – but just barely.

1 Corinthians 3:6-15 (The Message)

Planting and Harvesting in Today's Fields

I (Blake) didn't walk across the street. In my first appointment as a solo pastor in a small Arkansas congregation in a mid-sized town, I was under the mistaken impression that I was supposed to pastor the church – not much was said about the community. It was the 'second' United Methodist Church in town, and a fraction the size of the First Church, nestled in a neighborhood that also included an apartment complex. I was trained in the 'attractional model' of church growth that trusted that if you build it ('it' being nice buildings, great programs, and excellent worship), then they will inevitably come. The missional model of going out into the neighborhood mission field and being in ministry with the community was not yet articulated in ways that I could hear it and adapt my way leading the church. So I didn't walk across the street. I never modeled missional ministry nor the God-sized IMPACT that Christ can bring through deep and abiding missional relationships. It never came up, and I was never held accountable for it. We did manage okay. The church managed to grow – attendance actually doubled over a few years – but it was unsustainable growth which was not rooted in the community. Over a decade later, I regret not walking across the street from the church and actually being in relationship with our neighbors.

It is called a mission field for a reason. As Christ followers, we are planters of seeds – God's seeds. Many of us struggle from time to time with our seeds. Sometimes we hold onto the seeds, feeling ill-equipped or fearful to plant. Some of those seeds never have a chance to grow. They lie dormant. Other times, we plant seeds which will produce fruits we may never see. Ultimately, we are called as Christ followers to plant Christ's seeds consistently. When we plant seeds consistently, we will indeed see some of the fruits of God's seeds. Too many times we give up too early. Too many times we pass over the ripe fruit God planted because we ignore the seeds we have not personally planted. Too many times we do not see any new fruit; therefore, we quit planting. Other times, we leave the planting up to others. Even other times, we miss the most important part of planting seeds: the HARVEST. We are ALL called to plant Christ's seeds. Yes, ALL of us. Each and every one of us is called to IMPACT the world with Christ's love and grace. And we are not only a seed-planting people; we are also responsible for the harvesting. We are ALL responsible for the harvest. We are ALL responsible to walk across the room – to walk across the street. It is simple – *mature disciples* disciple others.

As a fourth-generation United Methodist, I (Kay) was taught evangelism. It was simple. Invite people to church! In today's church, we are left with Dr. Phil's famous question, "How's that working for you?" In the 1950s through the 1970s, that form of evangelism was somewhat effective. Because we lived in a church-centric world, people were more apt to accept an invitation to church. But in today's world, culture actually points people away from the church.

Most of us (both lay and clergy) were not equipped to practice evangelism for the modern times. At best, we were taught passive evangelism – do some really good deeds for people, and somehow, they will connect it back to the church and come to worship. Yet we were not equipped for active evangelism – building authentic relationships with the unchurched so that we might have the opportunity to share our faith. Sharing Christ (planting, nurturing, and harvesting) is our responsibility and our privilege as a Christ follower – a mature disciple.

The Questions

As the church, we are in the business of relationship building. Building our personal relationship with Christ and helping others get to know Christ and build a relationship. Again, many of us were often taught evangelism as a church invitation. Yet we have found this is not very effective in today's world. Instead, we must refocus our evangelism efforts towards relationships. The unchurched are not interested in your specific church as a starting point. Instead, people first want to know why you are a Christ follower. They want to know why you choose to believe – why you choose this lifestyle. We sometimes fear an unchurched person's first questions will be testing our Bible knowledge. This is most often not the case. While theology is vitally important, most unchurched folks simply are not equipped or interested in the theological debates that fill up so much of our time. People are looking for other people 'they can do life with.' The next stage of curiosity will likely be why being a part of a church is important. Then the person might be interested in knowing more about your church. See, we start with the third step when we invite people to church first. Unchurched folks want to know first why God, then why a church, and then finally why your church. In his book *Leading Beyond the Walls,*[4] Adam Hamilton offers three questions that every church leader needs to think through:

1. Why do people need Christ?

---

4 Hamilton, Adam. *Leading Beyond the Walls*. Nashville: Abingdon, 2002, pp. 21–30.

2. Why do people need the church?

3. Why do they need this particular church?

And then Hamilton adds a fourth question:

4. To whom does our church belong?

While the fourth question is not as critical for the unchurched, it is critically important for those in the church to know. Those of us inside the church must clearly understand to whom the church belongs. The church does not belong to the pastor, the lay leaders, the biggest giver, the longest-tenured folks, or even the congregation as a whole. The church belongs to Christ. As Christ followers, we gather to do the work of the church by planting seeds, fertilizing and watering the seeds, and harvesting the crop. We are the laborers – not the owners. When a congregation fully understands this, the potential IMPACT will be far greater!

The Stripping of Laity's Missional Ownership

As much as we now know the church belongs to Christ, we as laity also must take 'ownership' of the mission of the church. By taking ownership, we do not want to create a misunderstanding of terminology. Having ownership is about having complete buy-in and commitment. Ownership in the church is about 'owning' the mission of making disciples. Ownership is about taking responsibility for the church living out its purpose. Yet, over the past few decades, the laity have been stripped or have allowed the stripping of this missional ownership. In other words, the laity have allowed their responsibility and commitment to the mission to be taken away. Along the way, the church has become clergy-dependent, clergy-centric, and even professionalized. In too many cases, 'Ownership' has been reduced to making sure that nothing new ever happens. The laity have somehow come to the false conclusion that we 'hire' our ministry to be done for us. After all, isn't that why clergy exist and what we pay them for? The pastoral role has moved away from equipping to either autocratic leadership or a hireling mentality.

When a church is pastor-centric or personality-driven, the laity have become deprived of using their spiritual gifts for ministry. Laity are not given the opportunity to lead and grow in their faith. Often pastor-centric churches have high peaks and valleys of worship attendance. Ministry is dependent on the personality of a pastor. The laity are at the whim of the latest pastor's charisma, ministry passions, or interests. The church is not aligned with mission and vision. The culture of the community mission field is not relevant to the ministries of the church.

If there is a change in clergy leadership of a pastor-driven church, you will likely see a steep decline in worship attendance upon his/her departure. Likely, everything was dependent on the pastor's approval or leadership. The laity did not take 'ownership' in the ministry. It was simply the latest pastor's ministry for which the laity are spectators or (even worse) customers. We will address the complicated situation of pastoral transitions in Chapter Eight.

Our tribe (the United Methodist Church) was founded as a movement of the laity. Specifically, Methodism was originally designed as a discipling and missional society or 'parachurch' organization to accompany their membership in the Church of England, which was not meeting the challenges of the 'modern world' of the Eighteenth Century. In America, the Revolutionary War changed the trajectory of the Methodist Movement dramatically. A series of other decisions over the last two hundred years converted this lay-led parachurch movement into a clergy-dominated hierarchical church. Ironically, our denomination is having problems meeting the challenges of our 21st Century "modern world." Many churches have lost their way. We, as laity, must once again claim our roots while also reclaiming responsibility *for* and commitment *to* our church and God's Mission. The pastor-centric model is not effective and sustainable long-term. The laity movement where all members know their role as seed planters and harvesters is the most sustainable and effective method for reaching new people for Christ. To have an IMPACT in today's culture, we must have a renewal of the laity movement.

A Season Ripe for IMPACT

The church today has a remarkable opportunity as an instrument of Jesus Christ to make disciples and make a God-sized IMPACT upon the world. We have written this book because we believe that the mainline church is situated perfectly to share Christ's grace-filled vision in today's complex world. We are situated in a culture where there is a rise of skeptical 'nones' and cynical 'dones.' There is a deep desire today, especially among the generational Millennials, for authenticity, of experiences over the acquisition of stuff, and of relationships over authority. Followers of Jesus Christ understand what it means to have meaning in our lives; we know that we are sinners in need of grace, not inauthentic sanctified robots; and we believe that it is possible to make a God-sized IMPACT when we join together as a community of faith and a movement of the Holy Spirit.

The last point is important – it takes a community of

disciples to live into God's plan. And again, we believe that the rising generations are perfectly equipped to meet God's needs – if the church is willing to embrace them. Most of us were raised with a particular image of leadership. We were taught the 'Great Men' version of history, and most of our models of leadership have been shaped by decades of forceful (male) leaders seeking to persuade. We have valued and honored the Lone Ranger and the rugged individualist. Those models are sorely inadequate to meet the needs of today and tomorrow.

We will need to listen more and pontificate less, and we will need to build new partnerships and create communities wrapped around a clear purpose. Millennials have been raised up with different models of collaborative leadership that actually do a great job of meeting today's complex challenges if we can make space to adapt to their collaborative leadership models. Recently, I (Blake) remarked to my teenage daughter that she seemed to be doing quite a few group projects for school. We were looking at her schedule, and I saw several in-depth group projects every month, and I thought back, realizing that I had one, perhaps two, group projects my whole high school career. This put into perspective all the articles I have read lately about modern offices in Silicon Valley with communal workspaces and project nooks instead of private offices. The rising generation is built and equipped for community effort. Can the church make space in its lay governance and clergy systems to celebrate Millennials' amazing gifts for community-building around shared purpose?

Planning Your IMPACT

Questions for the Lay Leadership/Board Member

- As leaders, how prepared are you to answer Adam Hamilton's four questions:

    1. Why do people need Christ?

    2. Why do people need the church?

    3. Why do they need this particular church?

    4. To whom does our church belong?

- Discuss the leadership models in your church. How are important decisions made? How clear are the roles and expectations for clergy, staff, lay leaders? What, if any, adjustments might need to be made?

- Discuss specifically how the Millennial generation's leadership models might affect the current church leadership culture.

Questions for the Disciple

- Describe your understanding of the responsibility as a Christ follower in planting and harvesting seeds.

- Share your thoughts on the type of clergy and leadership models that are practiced in your church. What, if any, adjustments need to be made?

Questions for the Pastors and Staff

- Discuss the leadership models in your church.

- How would you describe the balance of authority in the clergy/lay partnership?

- How clear are the roles and expectations for clergy, staff, and lay leaders? What, if any, adjustments might need to be made?

- How is staff helping equip laity to answer Adam Hamilton's four questions?

Chapter Two

Cultural Impact: Creating Ripples in the Lake

While Paul waited for them in Athens, he was deeply distressed to find that the city was flooded with idols. He began to interact with the Jews and Gentile God-worshippers in the synagogue. He also addressed whoever happened to be in the marketplace each day. Certain Epicurean and Stoic philosophers engaged him in discussion too. Some said, "What an amateur! What's he trying to say?" Others remarked, "He seems to be a proclaimer of foreign gods." (They said this because he was preaching the good news about Jesus and the resurrection.) They took him into custody and brought him to the council on Mars Hill. "What is this new teaching? Can we learn what you are talking about? You've told us some strange things and we want to know what they mean." (They said this because all Athenians as well as the foreigners who live in Athens used to spend their time doing nothing but talking about or listening to the newest thing.) Paul stood up in the middle of the council on Mars Hill and said, "People of Athens, I see that you are very religious in every way. As I was walking through town and carefully observing your objects of worship, I even found an altar with this inscription: 'To an unknown God.' What you worship as unknown, I now proclaim to you ..."

Acts 17:16-23 (Common English Bible)

21

Looking at the landscape of United Methodism along-side recent statistical demographics, I am reminded John Wesley said "the world is my parish." Yet, by and large, we don't even own our own neighborhoods. How do we, as Jesus' disciples, IMPACT our culture, and how aware are we when our culture is impacting us? In the scripture from Acts chapter 17, Paul is trying to figure out how to connect to a very different audience. His first reaction is 'distress' because all he saw in Athens was that, in Eugene Peterson's *The Message* paraphrase, "the city was a junkyard of idols." While rarely made of marble, we in 21st Century America certainly still have our idols, and we put all sorts of things – people, ideologies, political commitments, money, and 'stuff' – on pedestals. Our checking account registers and a cursory view of how we spend our time would most certainly distress St. Paul just as much as ancient Athens' junkyard of idols! But 2000 years ago, Paul managed to get past his distress and do what Jesus still calls us to do: get out and connect with people – in both the religious centers and marketplaces. In order to be effective, we have to do what Paul did – learn about the culture and the people to whom Jesus calls us to witness.

In American culture, especially in the white middle-class southern and midwestern subcultures that formed the authors of this book, the church had it easy, and we let our evangelism muscles deteriorate. Everything in our culture was designed to put behinds in pews on Sunday morning. Church membership was socially *required,* not just socially acceptable. Blue laws gave the church a monopoly on folk's non-working time. Protestant prayers were standard in public schools. The 'Leave It To Beaver' model for family life created a huge volunteer workforce of strong, smart women whose outlet to channel their spiritual gifts often became community service, particularly in the church.

But the era of cultural Christendom is over. The United Methodist Church, along with other mainline denominations, has been shrinking for two generations. One of our difficulties is that we kept some of Christendom's assumptions and traditions around like household idols. Now, as we are trying to share the saving grace of Christ in a new day in a very complicated culture, these idols are getting in the way of Christ's message and our potential IMPACT. A few years ago, I (Blake) invited Jim Ozier, our congregational development colleague, to visit with a troubled and shrinking congregation seeking to possibly connect to a larger church in the city. They had turned inward over the years, with many members having moved away or to newer parts of town, and only a faithful few left in the building in a part of the city with a huge need. He read their grieving hearts and knew the difficult decisions they had ahead of them and simply said, "You know, sometimes the culture and community change so fast the church just can't keep up." There were nods all around the room, and even a few tears. That was the perfect pastoral response to this particular congregation's situation. It really was time for them to let go and try something new, and with a new congregational partner in ministry, they have been able to do just that! But at *that* moment, I also knew that thousands of our congregations across the country have simply not been able to keep up with the changes in our communities.

Since both of us (Kay and Blake) spend most of our time coaching and equipping United Methodist congregations, we have found it helpful to connect to our Eighteenth Century spiritual DNA when we encourage congregations to reconnect to their communities. John Wesley, the primary founder of Methodism, may have led a group nicknamed the Bible Moths, but they were never content to remain safely behind the Oxford University gates in their small group study. Certainly, they studied scripture, examined their souls, celebrated the sacraments, and encouraged spiritual accountability, but these Methodists also visited the debtors' prisons, opened orphanages, started schools, and cared for the poor. They exerted political influence, such as seeking the abolition of slavery in England. Early Methodists in America followed this tradition of compassion and justice, founding hospitals and universities, advocating for temperance and against sweatshops and child labor. Our very Methodist DNA includes caring for our communities. We have a deep history of making an IMPACT in individual souls, in our communities, across our nation, and even around the world. Yet we have allowed this legacy of the Wesley Brother's Bible Moths and the early Methodists to get dusty and moth-ridden. We have lost our desire and the muscles to IMPACT our culture.

IMPACT Ripples

When I (Blake) was a boy scout, we often went to a camp by a large lake in Arkansas. I loved to get up a bit early, start the fire, and skip rocks on the lake. The early morning was the best time to skip rocks. The lake was still and quiet, with every ripple from my stones causing ripples in the water. I would spend some time finding just the right rocks – flat ones that would skip well – and would try my best to see how many times the rock would skip, each skip causing an impact that would make ripples in the water. Later in the day, the lake would be filled with boats and swimmers and waves and commotion, and I would have great difficulty seeing the ripples of my skipping stones. But the morning was all mine, and I would choose only the best stones. Today, churches are like my experience of trying and failing to skip stones in the middle of the day. We church leaders would rather have the busy-ness of today's culture return to the calm to the church-centric cultural of the 1950s and 1960s. Churches struggle to see their ripple effect in today's world with the chaos of our busy, frantic lives added to the inward-facing focus of most churches.

Our post-Christendom culture is a *really* busy lake – actually, it is quite the diverse and crowded marketplace of ideas, much like Paul found in Athens. Our supply of good skipping rocks is limited. Ministries that seemed to be fruitful just a few years ago are struggling; giving patterns have changed, along with worship frequency even amongst the most faithful. In a busy lake with few good stones left lying around on our shores, the ripples of our IMPACT are becoming more and more difficult to discern.

So, what's YOUR culture?

Both Arkansas and Pennsylvania, where we each serve in ministry, depend upon the agriculture industry. The United Methodist Church, over two centuries, built a church in every little town and village. Basically, our churches are a horse-ride away from each other, and most people in our states lived far outside our few major cities. A whole pipeline was created to place clergy in 'nice little churches' across the countryside. But times have changed. Agricultural work in the United States has fallen 80% in the last 60 years.[5] This is due to a

---

5 Thompson, Derek, "Where Did All the Workers Go? 60 Years of Economic Change in 1 Graph," *The Atlantic.* January 26, 2012. http://www.theatlantic.com/business/archive/2012/01/where-did-all-the-workers-go-60-years-of-economic-change-in-1-graph/252018/.

variety of factors, including farming equipment technology and efficiency. Most of our church members have seen their small towns shrink to even smaller towns or simply disappear because a few people and some equipment can now do the work that required dozens of people a short time ago. Those 'nice little churches' for a full-time pastor are quickly disappearing during the adult lifetimes of their members. In short, a single generation of church leaders have seen the churches their great-grandparents built diminish from full pews to empty husks.

Their pastoral leadership went from being seminary trained and ordained elders to licensed local pastors to bi-vocational pastors commuting to the church to leadership by a layperson in the community. Part of this is related to the cost of clergy, which continues to rise, especially due to housing and healthcare expenses, which places a strain on the fewer families in the congregation. As a connectional church with an appointed clergy, the United Methodist Church is often the last mainline church presence in the rural town or maybe even the county. In too many small-town churches, members are wondering, *Who will be the last one to turn off the lights once everyone has passed away?* Small-town congregations that have unlocked more lay-led models of missional engagement have had the most success in charting a new way. Instead of waiting for (and spending 80% of their budget on) 'the next preacher,' they have used their resources for community engagement.

I (Kay) had the great privilege of walking alongside a small church that was blown away by a tornado. Yet the small church was set on rebuilding. With some persistent prodding from judicatory leaders, the congregation finally decided to rebuild a modern structure rather than the original structure built in the 1960s. Once the new building was built, the congregation was sure people would flock to the new facility. Yet this did not happen. Instead, the congregation that returned to the building was smaller than ever. The church took on a transformational process specifically for small churches. They readily agreed on the recommendations presented during the consultation. However, the congregation struggled to find the energy and momentum to carry out the recommendations. Soon, it was evident the conversation needed to turn to legacy. While the decision was very difficult, the church made the decision that the most faithful way forward was for them to turn over their new facility and the $100,000 left in the bank to allow something new to happen to reach new people. And indeed, that is exactly just what happened. A planter was brought in, and a year later, the church launched with two services and more than 300 people. This legacy congregation of fewer than forty people made way for a younger, more diverse congregation of new believers to emerge at The Light in Joplin, Missouri, led by Pastor Andrew Moyer. What an incredible story of faithful people allowing God's preferred future to shine!

Meanwhile, when I (Blake) visited Chicago for a denominational training and equipping event, I heard that 30% of Chicago residents speak a language other than English at home, 130 languages are spoken in the Chicago School System, there are more Iraqi Christians in Chicago than in Iraq, and only Poland has more Poles. Congregations like the Urban Village Church, a multisite church in Chicago, have responded to their complex culture by staying flexible. The congregation is built upon a community organizing model and owns no worship facilities but, instead, gathers in theaters and other locations based upon demographic studies and Chicago's public transit stops.

There never actually was a single 'American Culture,' but the church has tried hard over decades to make churches (and particularly their pastors) generic enough to make pastoral appointments easier. But regardless if your existing culture is urban or rural, diverse or monochromatic, there are some huge shifts coming that will impact 'the way things have always been' in your community. In 2015, the U.S. Census gave us some updated information about how our nation looks like and will look like. According to the report, *Projections of the Size and Composition of the U.S. Population: 2014 to 2060.*[6] Here are some of their conclusions:

- The U.S. population is expected to grow more slowly in future decades than it did in the previous century.

- Around the time the 2020 Census is conducted, more than half of the nation's children are expected to be part of a minority race or ethnic group.

- The U.S. population as a whole is expected to follow a similar trend, becoming majority-minority in 2044. The minority population is projected to rise to 56 percent of the total in 2060, compared with 38 percent in 2014.

- A major milestone will be achieved by the 2030 Census: all Baby Boomers will have reached age 65 or older (this will actually occur in 2029). Consequently, in that year, one in five Americans would be 65 or older, up from one in seven in 2014.

- By 2060, the nation's foreign-born population would reach nearly 19 percent of the total population, up from 13 percent in 2014.

Economically speaking, a Pew Report from December

---

6 See the Census press release at https://www.census.gov/newsroom/press-releases/2015/cb15-tps16.html. The complete census report from 2015 is at https://www.census.gov/library/publications/2015/demo/p25-1143.html

2015[7] shares that "After more than four decades of serving as the nation's economic majority, the American middle class is now matched in number by those in the economic tiers above and below it." This report also states that the number of people living in households inside the lowest income segment is increasing, moving from 16% in 1970 to 20% today. Our mission field is changing! Meanwhile, our United Methodist denomination, which had evolved into a primarily (90%) Caucasian middle-class church over the last century, statistically mirroring the nation at large, is shrinking. And, of course, we are in 'good' company, with most mainline and evangelical Protestant churches also experiencing similar issues of decline.

There are also huge changes in generational identity and outlook. A 2017 Barna Study has shown that "The percentage of Gen Z [born between 1999 to 2015] that identifies as atheist is double that of the U.S. general adult population."[8] Talk about the *nones* (those who select 'none' on religious identity surveys) and the *dones* (those who have given up on church[9]) has begun to pervade conversation amongst church leaders, but there is a lot more generational transformation going on than changes in church interactions. While both Millennials and Baby Boomers have become lovely punching bags, most congregational leaders have done little research on rising generations beyond

---

7 Pew Research Center, *The American Middle Class Is Losing Ground.* December 9, 2015. See http://www.pewsocialtrends.org/2015/12/09/the-american-middle-class-is-losing-ground/. See more excellent studies about change, demographics, and culture at http://www.pewsocialtrends. org/.

8 Barna Group, "Atheism Doubles Among Generation Z," *Research Releases in Millennials and Generations.* January 24, 2018. https://www.barna.com/research/atheism-doubles-among-generation-z/

9 For more about the 'dones,' a helpful book is Josh Packard's and Ashleigh Hope's *Church refugees: sociologists reveal why people are done with the church but not their faith.* Loveland, Colorado: Group, 2015.

reading the latest version of "Top Ten Reasons Millennials Hate Your Church" posts on Facebook (by the way, the millennial children of this book's authors have informed us that Facebook is just for 'old people'). While we worry about the economic sustainability of our ecclesiastical institutions, we rarely acknowledge that Millennials have enormous economic anxiety. Home ownership is out of reach for most Millennials because of structural changes in the economy.[10] The cost of a college education and health care has skyrocketed past average inflation, and those Millennials who hit the job market during the recession will have their earnings reduced their entire lives. Millennials are delaying marriage & child raising. Many from Generation X have assumed their entire lives that they would be the first generation of Americans to be worse off than their parents.[11] And let's not forget about the Boomers! Another Pew Research study has found that the divorce rate of Boomers has doubled in the last few years, a trend called 'gray divorce.'[12]

As you can tell, the lake in which we are trying to skip our stones is already experiencing quite a lot of waves. It is getting terribly difficult to create some God-sized ripples of our own when so much of culture is already being impacted by all of today's changes. But, of course, there is still more.

---

10 Oyedele, Akin, "6 reasons why more millennials aren't buying homes," *Business Insider.* June 5, 2017. http://www.businessinsider.com/millennial-homeownership-lower-2017-6. Also, the longform Huffington Post article and art project by Michael Hobbes, "Millennials are Screwed," at http://highline.huffingtonpost.com/articles/en/poor-Millennials/ offers a creative and eye-opening study of millennial economic anxiety.

11 Woodruff, Mandy. "Not Doing Better Than Their Parents: The Stunning Fall Of Generation X." *Business Insider,* AOL.com. May 30, 2013. https://www.aol.com/2013/05/30/generation-x-worse-off-than-parents-recession/; Hymowitz, Carol. "Generation X has it worse than baby boomers, millennials." Bloomberg News. June 10, 2015. https://www.bostonglobe.com/business/2015/06/10/Millennials-think-they-have-bad-generation-has-worse/3vhfpB2PCGOSHD-2mEX1AwM/story.html

12 Stepler, Renee. "Led by Baby Boomers, divorce rates climb for America's 50+ population." *Fact Tank: News In the Numbers.* Pew Research Center. March 9, 2017. http://www.pewresearch.org/fact-tank/2017/03/09/led-by-baby-Boomers-divorce-rates-climb-for-americas-50-population/

In addition to the changing demographics and macroeco-
nomic forces bringing change to the corner of the lake that
is your church's American subculture, the digital revolution
is certainly creating its own wake. And it is a big one! My
(Blake's) academic background includes a master's degree
in historical theology, with a focus on the medieval and
Reformation eras (please don't laugh). One of the tidbits of
historical data that I had not previously appreciated is how
much of the Protestant Reformation five hundred years
ago was enabled by the invention of a paradigm-shifting
technology of information-sharing and social media: Guten-
berg's movable type printing press. Without the printing
press, Martin Luther would have probably lived and died
an obscure monk in Germany who had caused a little local
trouble. We are a people of the Word, and now words move
at the speed of light. The moveable type press created new
pathways for information to be discovered, shared, and
promoted. Ideas quickly became movements, and movements
changed the world. We now know what happened the last
time that information technology took a great leap. To imagine that today's digital technology and social media has no
effect on the larger culture would be foolish. To pretend that
the church would never be affected by the digital revolution
would be both foolish and terribly unwise. In John Wesley's
Journal dated April 2, 1739, he wrote: "At four in the after-
noon, I submitted to be more vile, and proclaimed in the
highways the glad tidings of salvation, speaking from a little
eminence in a ground adjoining to the city, to about three
thousand people."[13]   There is no doubt in our minds that

---

13 Wesley, John, "The Journal of John Wesley, April 2, 1739," in *The Works of John Wesley,
Third Edition, Complete and Unabridged, Vol. I: Journals from October 14, 1735 to November
29, 1745,* ed. T. Jackson. London: Wesleyan Methodist Book Room, 1831, 1872. Reprinted:
Grand Rapids: Baker Book House, 1978. Page 185.

John and Charles Wesley would have jumped at the chance to use every media avenue, every new technology, and every social media platform (even the 'vile' ones like Twitter) to share the message of Christ's grace in order to make a God-sized IMPACT on today's culture.

While pastors and denominational officials fret, we laity don't talk much about these huge demographic and economic shifts, which are all connected to larger cultural shifts. If we do, rarely do we connect these issues to what is going on in our pews and Sunday School classrooms.

Impact Ripples In Choppy Waters?

When we do start talking about these changes in the church, we usually look at it all from the congregation's point of view. We are usually asking, "How will all this change impact the sustainability of our church?" Or worse, we ask, "How will we keep our church budget in the black?" We challenge you to flip the script! Imagine looking at these changes from the point of view of the person without a church home. Even better, what if we were to look at this from the point of view of our neighbors who don't yet know the love of grace of Jesus Christ! Some of these changes may be challenging their lives and livelihood. So, instead of asking questions of institutional sustainability, ask, "How can we have a God-sized IMPACT in people's lives, as together we are affected by all these changes?" How will we connect with and IMPACT the souls of Millennials working in a short-term 'gig economy' with no realistic plan for home ownership or a long-term career? How will we connect with and IMPACT the souls of the enormous numbers of divorced Baby Boomers who have seen their lives change drastically right before retirement? Middle-class families with a stay-at-home mom, 2.5 kids, and a minivan in the garage are no longer the statistical reality for our mission field (and really we must be honest that this description has left WAY too many people out for generations). How shall we adapt our ministries to meet the deepest spiritual needs of actual people in our communities today?

Creating ripples from your IMPACT starts with making sure that the lake actually has some water in it. We church folks are great at being busy, but we are often trying to skip stones in a lake that has been drained (drained of resources, energy, and the understanding that we are called to do whatever it takes to reach our neighbors for Christ). We ache for the culture to once again be like it was two generations ago. Church folk complain about how traveling sports on weekends has cut into their young families' worship attendance, but we never visit the soccer fields to see how we can bless and IMPACT the families there. We find many congregations spend more of their time fussing over the changing culture (and how they don't like it) rather than adapting the ministries of the church to meet the culture of our communities. We desire to 'do church' on the calm morning pond full of quiet water when this is simply not the reality for most all our churches. What would it take for your church to show up at your neighborhood pond and decide to create ripple effects for IMPACT no matter the condition of the pond?

Planning Your IMPACT

Questions for the Lay Leadership/Board Member

- What is your church's current ripple effect on your community culture?

- What could be the ripple effect on your community that could provide the largest potential IMPACT?

- What are the first two steps in closing the gap between your current missional ripples and your potential IMPACT?

Questions for the Disciple

- What is your personal ripple effect on your neighborhood?

- What is one thing you could do to IMPACT the culture of your community for Jesus Christ?

- How might one person be impacted by the ripples that could come from your actions?

Questions for the Pastor and Staff

- How are you helping your congregation have a realistic and holistic understanding of American culture as a whole, your regional culture, and your church's mission field?

- What next steps will you take to help your congregation more fully understand their culture and the potential ripples of their IMPACT?

- What equipping is necessary with your leaders to help them in this reality check and new understanding?

Chapter Three

IMPACT starts with Discipleship

Now the eleven disciples went to Galilee, to the mountain where Jesus told them to go. When they saw him, they worshipped him, but some doubted. Jesus came near and spoke to them, "I've received all authority in heaven and on earth. Therefore, go and make disciples of all nations, baptizing them in the name of the Father and of the Son and of the Holy Spirit, teaching them to obey everything that I've commanded you. Look, I myself will be with you every day until the end of this present age."

Matthew 28:16-20 (Common English Bible)

We have gotten ourselves a bit confused when it comes to discipleship. What is discipleship? What is its purpose? How would I know when I am a disciple? A mature disciple? Once you have started attending worship regularly, does that 'make' you a disciple? Once you become a member of a church, does that 'make' you a disciple? Once you have completed Disciple I and Disciple II classes, are you a disciple now? If you attend Sunday school regularly, are you a disciple? If you serve on a missions project, are you then a disciple? Pastors and theologians have spent hours upon hours debating its very meaning. No wonder our congregations are confused!

According to the official United Methodist website, a disciple is defined as:

> **The active living of the individual Christian in accordance with the teachings of Jesus Christ, that is, being as effective a disciple of Christ as possible. Discipleship involves a ministry of outreaching love and witness to others concerning Christ and God's grace. Discipleship also calls the Christian to ministries of servanthood and service to the world to the glory of God and for human fulfillment.[14]**

This definition is a great explanation of what a disciple *does*. However, discipleship is not just about doing certain things. Discipleship is a way of *being*. Discipleship is an ever-growing relationship with Jesus Christ and the intentional lifestyle to be more Christ-like every day. It is through disciples that we will IMPACT God's world. Without intentional discipleship, we are a people who attend a gathering of well-intentioned people who desire to do nice things. Again, we have the best of intentions but are simply not *intentional*. There is a better and more faithful way.

---

14 The UMC.org website's "What we believe" section is sourced to Alan K Waltz's *A Dictionary for United Methodists*. Nashville: Abingdon Press, 1991. See http://www.umc.org/what-we-believe/glossary-discipleship.

From Membership to Discipleship to IMPACT

Membership in a congregation is different from discipleship. Membership is about institutional connection. One can be a member of a country club or a member of a professional society. As disciples, we are followers of Jesus Christ and members of the Body of Christ, the church. Membership in a church is certainly important; it is the Christian's way of living out Christ's calling in the community and practicing our faith commitment for the transformation of the world. Membership in a church, then, is the communal element of the larger faith journey that is Christian discipleship. In the United Methodist Church, we clearly separate our sacramental baptism ritual (Christ IN us) from the vows of church membership (Christ working THROUGH us). We do the work of discipleship a great disservice whenever we reduce discipleship to the expectations of institutional membership in a local church or denomination.

In working with churches, we have seen many churches conflate the process of making disciples with the vows of membership. In the United Methodist Church, most people joined by pledging their 'prayers, presence, gifts, and service.' In 2008, the international General Conference of the United Methodist Church added a fifth vow of 'witness,' an excellent addition that affirms the expectation of laity for IMPACT. We have heard, and I (Blake) have preached, way too many four- or five-part sermon series in October (stewardship month, of course!) on the vows of membership. I (Blake) also worked with a church that had previously created a whole second tier of membership (called 'Disciples' at that congregation) that took the four existing membership vows of that era and defined them with clearer expectations. The congregation then invited its existing members to 'level up' by signing an annual covenant to be 'Disciples.' Only 'Disciples' who signed would be considered for roles on the church's board and committees. A lapel pin was even included for those members who are 'Disciples.' While I applaud the intention behind this strategy – higher expectation churches do indeed have a higher level of overall commitment and impact – the approach created several problems.

When I arrived and surveyed the situation, I noticed a few things: First, there was still, years later, an enormous amount of internal conflict over this tactic. Second, the clarified expectations were all focused on the needs of the church as an institution, not the spiritual growth or discipleship journey of the individual Christ follower. Third, the mix of internal conflict, division of members into groups (with corresponding lapel pins), and institutional self-focus had poisoned the idea of high expectation membership and even poisoned the word 'disciple' in the congregation.

The suggestion for this church was to not only 'disappear' all the signage related to the policy but to begin creating an intentional discipleship system that focused on the faith journey of the individual and her IMPACT.

When people are being discipled, when they are growing in faith, and when they are making a transformative impact in their community and the world, the institution will always be fine. To focus first (or only) on the institution invites not only cynicism but also a loss of the great, sacramental, grace-filled journey of discipleship that is Christ's gift to the church.

Linking Stewardship and Discipleship

In a study of one congregation's history, I (Blake) discovered that every recent movement to 'make (better) disciples' had originated with the finance committee. Again and again, the church's budget crunch led to a conversation about stewardship, which led to a conversation about discipleship. While it is certainly true that committed, mature Christ followers are probably more generous, the purpose of making disciples of the Risen Christ is NOT ultimately to solve the financial worries of the institutional church. While the committee meant well, the composition of the finance committee was not well-suited to build the intentional discipleship pathway the congregation needed to make a God-sized IMPACT. Furthermore, the congregation saw through the attempts, and it made the entire church leadership look inauthentic.

What, then, should be the relationship between stewardship and discipleship? First, the expectations around Christian generosity should be rooted in a holistic view of a disciple's journey, with an expectation that a disciple's stewardship of all of God's gifts and one's generosity grows as the disciple's relationship with Christ deepens. Second, we need to recognize that stewardship and generosity are spiritual gifts, and God's gifts are expressed uniquely in every soul. Third, we must acknowledge that there have been huge shifts in Americans' giving patterns over the last decade and not expect our inherited institutional systems and expectations surrounding stewardship to drive us to make assumptions or quick judgments about the generosity or spirituality of others.

Americans are more generous than ever, but our methods of giving and the recipients of our gifts have changed dramatically. Secular non-profits and parachurch organizations have grown dramatically, especially since their ability to have a laser focus, outline their limited purpose, and communicate their outcomes connect to today's givers' desires for targeted giving. In comparison, the church's wide list of purposes, its dependence on the relational community for action, and its mission to "make disciples for the transformation of the world" seems vague and institutional. Filling out an annual stewardship card simply isn't connecting with the expectations or hopes of the rising generations. And as church leaders, we need to build a culture of celebration and thanksgiving when people do give. For example, a system needs to be in place for a pastor or staff member to thank every first time giver, to ensure that their giving, and (more importantly) their discipleship journey, continues to develop and grow. When we take people's giving for granted, we are taking their discipleship for granted.

Placing all the work for stewardship on the pastor's shoulders feeds into negative stereotypes about clergy and is a dereliction of duty by us as laity, so it is time for lay leadership to take responsibility for the overall stewardship plan, not just the expense lines of the annual church budget. The laity can help create a culture of generosity by first being generous personally. Second, the laity can help by being open to sharing their stories about growing in their generosity and even struggles in their tithing. Third, the laity can be a voice to teach, preach, model, and share about the importance of being generous with our time, talent, and treasures.

Once stewardship and generosity are placed in the context of a holistic understanding of discipleship, and the making of disciples is connected to the IMPACT focus of the congregation, then giving can be linked directly to that God-sized IMPACT that is the vision of the congregation. In linking together stewardship, the larger discipleship journey, and the congregation's IMPACT, don't forget that the story needs to be told again and again. As lay members, we need to share inside and outside the church the ways that God is doing amazing work through our church. IMPACT needs to be celebrated! These are God's stories! We must take it upon ourselves as laity to tell the pastor and staff of 'glory sightings' – when God is making a difference in people's lives and transforming the fabric of communities. This approach is authentic, Christ-centered, and rooted in both the individual experience of grace and the calling we have as disciples to transform our communities and world. To connect all these dots, the congregation's next step is to create an intentional discipleship pathway.

Intentional Discipleship Pathways

Having an intentional pathway for discipleship is a must for each and every church if we are to help grow in our discipleship. A system, pathway, or a process allows us to be more intentional in helping people grow in their discipleship. Unfortunately, without an intentional plan, we find churches struggling to help their attenders and members grow in their discipleship.

Again, we have the best of intentions, but without an intentional plan, we are destined to have pews filled with consumers rather than disciples. We are doomed to be an inwardly-focused church without a sent-out people to disciple others and transform the world.

41

As churches struggle with intentional discipleship, there is a plethora of resources that have been created or shared in the past few years. There seems to be an emerging conversation about intentional discipleship systems as more and more churches struggle with developing disciples.

Even with this renewed focus and numerous resources, churches continue to struggle to identify their intentional faith development plan. Or, at the very least, churches are seeing little traction or results from their discipleship process. As churches, we continue to grapple with this very hard work of making disciples – the very Great Commission Jesus gave us!

Junius Dotson, General Secretary of Discipleship Ministries for the United Methodist Church, has been leading a new conversation in our denomination about intentional faith development. Dotson offers this insight in regards to intentional faith development:

> *Whether you know it or not, you already have a discipleship system in place in your church. Your current system produces exactly what it is designed to produce. Once we begin to think about our church as a system, we can start to think intentionally about what our system is producing. Intentional discipleship means we know and have planned out the many ways that people new to the faith enter into our church's discipleship system and move through it on their way to growth and maturity. We then clearly communicate the opportunities that disciples have through the church, and offer ways to self-assess and reflect upon the next steps for their spiritual journey. Our hope is that as churches and conferences think intentionally, we will begin to chip away at discipleship by osmosis – "We don't really know: People show up, things happen, and somehow, disciples are formed." [15]*

So, every church has a discipleship pathway ... a few even

---

15 Dotson, Junius B. *Developing an Intentional Discipleship System: A Guide for Congregations.* Nashville: Discipleship Ministries, 2017, pp 24–25.

have an intentional one. In our experience, most churches we have worked with across the nation do not have an *intentional* system or plan. I (Kay) can probably count on one hand the number of churches I have worked with over the past decade who had an intentional faith development process when I walked in the door. Friends, this struggle is real, and we must address this core fundamental aspect of our Christian walk.

In Kay's book, *Gear Up,* she explains the 'bookends' to a discipleship plan.[16] Prior to the discipleship pathway, the church exhibits processes of hospitality (meeting new people and first impressions) and connection (building relationships with one another). Only once we have relationships with one another can we help connect and move people along the discipleship pathway. A discipleship pathway must eventually lead people to disciple others – to become a missionary to reach new people for Christ. Disciples make disciples. Discipleship mobilizes laity for IMPACT! Without those intentional bookend processes, the discipleship process is incomplete.

Now let's explore what a discipleship pathway is and what needs to be included. An intentional process must be purposeful. There is an endgame in mind. This pathway has an intended destination. There is a transformation that is expected. There is a different way of being and living as a result of moving along on the pathway. Discipleship is participatory. It is experiential. It is IMPACTFUL!

Discipleship is not just about learning the 'head stuff.' Discipleship includes the knowledge of discipleship but also

---

16 Kotan, Kay. *Gear Up!: Nine Essential Processes For The Optimized Church.* Nashville: Abingdon Press, 2017.

encompasses the change in heart and the resulting changes in attitude, experiences, and how one goes about daily life. Too often churches have a false belief that offering the right number of educational classes for the right amount of time will magically produce mature disciples.

Sadly, we know the outcome of this process. We have churches of people stuffed full of Christian knowledge without the purpose of being a mature follower of Jesus Christ, much less disciples who are sent out to transform the world and share Jesus Christ with others.

There are several excellent examples and resources to assist you in creating your church's own intentional faith development process. In addition to the new Discipleship Ministries resources related to the See All The People campaign, some of our favorites that seem to be effective in helping churches develop their discipleship pathways are the books *Stride: Creating a Discipleship Pathway for Your Church* by Ken Willard and Mike Schreiner, *Membership to Discipleship* by Phil Maynard, and *Journey 101: Steps to the Life God Intends* by Church of the Resurrection staff Carol Cartmill, Jeff Kirby, and Michelle Kirby.

During my (Blake's) tenure as Executive Pastor at St. James United Methodist Church, a large membership congregation in Little Rock, I worked with a host of people, especially the then-Director of Faith Development, Kim Anderson, to create the framework for a church-wide discipleship pathway. We adapted the descriptions of different aspects of discipleship from Church of the Resurrection's excellent Journey 101 resources.[17]

---

17 Cartmill, Carol, Kirby, Jeff, and Kirby Michelle. Journey 101: *Knowing God, Loving God, And Serving God, Steps To The Life God Intends.* Nashville: Abingdon, 2013.

The 15 core traits of a deeply-committed Christian were identified by the authors, and together, these traits describe the discipleship path as a journey of Knowing, Loving, and Serving God. We reverse-engineered these traits into a chart to account for the earlier stages of discipleship maturation and spiritual growth based on a study of the writings of Phil Maynard and Greg Hawkins, the author of *MOVE*. This chart then became a guidepost for the church to begin rethinking all of its ministries.

The resulting chart is a tool to help individual disciples discern their current place on the pathway of discipleship and consider next steps to move closer to Christ and mature in their discipleship. Small group leaders, lay leaders, pastors, and church staff can also use this chart to assess their balance of ministries, make choices in curriculum and areas of emphasis, and make strategic decisions on the potential impact of disciples.

Of course a chart is not a discipleship path – it is simply one element of a much larger church-wide emphasis on the disciple-making mission of a congregation. The destination is clear – Christ-centered disciples. It also acknowledges that people mature unevenly as disciples, we backslide, and we have spiritual 'blind spots' like the rich young ruler.[18]

---

18 Mark 10:17–27

		Believing In Christ	Growing In Christ	Close To Christ	Christ-Centered
		First steps for those who desire to learn more about the Christian faith, the Church, and God.	Believer growing in Christ primarily through large group experiences while developing a heart for the needs of others.	Spiritually mature disciple who desires a deeper level of shared discipleship with others and seeks ways to unselfishly serve.	Deeply committed disciple who surrenders to God, reproduces the Christian faith in the life of others, lives a life of service.
KNOWING GOD	Christian Essentials	Is aware of the very basic beliefs of the Christian faith.	Seeks out ways to know more about Christ, the history of the Christian Tradition, and how to have a relationship with God.	Incorporates Christian creeds and beliefs into my faith walk and relationship with God.	Can share the gospel intelligently with non-Christians and nominally Christian friends.
	Bible Knowledge	Acknowledges the Bible is important, but the Bible is not yet a part of my everyday life.	Begins to explore the Bible as the inspired Word of God and understand its importance through small group or Sunday School classes.	Understands the grand sweep of the Bible's story of salvation, including a basic timeline of Biblical events, and applies its teachings in life.	Understands the Bible and knows how to interpret it as a guide and companion for life's journey.
	Church/ Methodist	Believes the church is a way to grow as a guide and companion for life's journey.	Begins to understand the importance of regular participation in the life of the church community.	Seeks to grow in understanding of the teachings of the universal church and the tenets of the United Methodist Church.	Committed to the local, connectional, and universal church and is committed to Christian unity even when opinions differ.
	Basic Christian Ethics	Understands and applies general Christian principles to everyday life. Tries to be a "good person."	Continues to grow in awareness of how the Christian faith impacts my life not just on Sunday but every day of the week.	Seeks to grow in understanding & applying Christian ethics through Bible study, worship, and conversations with other Christians.	Understands how to apply my Christian faith to important ethical issues. Is committed to living out Christian ethical principles.
	Knowing God's Will	Is aware but struggles with acknowledging and understanding God's will for my life.	Seeks to acknowledge God's will for my individual life and begins to follow the path.	Develops a growing discernment process for God's will in individual lives.	Has a growing sense of how to discern God's will for my life through prayer, Bible study and wisdom from other Christians.

		Believing In Christ	Growing In Christ	Close To Christ	Christ-Ce...
		First steps for those who desire to learn more about the Christian faith, the Church, and God.	*Believer growing in Christ primarily through large group experiences while developing a heart for the needs of others.*	*Spiritually mature disciple who desires a deeper level of shared discipleship with others and seeks ways to unselfishly serve.*	*Deeply committed disciple who surrenders to God, reproduces the Christian faith in the life of others, lives a life of service.*
LOVING GOD	Surrender	Acknowledges and realizes that God is in my life, but struggles to turn control of life over to God.	Begins to seek God's direction and will in my life through prayer, Bible study and worship.	Repents of sin, sets aside own desires. Surrenders more of self to God's will and plan.	Surrenders control of all aspects of my life to Jesus, repents of sin, sets aside personal desires & sense of importance. Offers my life in obedient service to God.
	Transformation	Moved to accept Christ by the Holy Spirit.	Seeks to grow in faith through regular participation in worship, small groups, and missions	Values and priorities are guided and shaped by the Holy Spirit.	Is continually transformed by the power of the Holy Spirit. Senses His power molding my values, priorities, and relationships into more Christ-like patterns.
	Spiritual Disciplines	Attends church occasionally, thinks about prayer more than actually praying, buys study books.	Begins regularly exploring spiritual life through prayer, Bible Study, and worship.	Prays daily, worships often, and is engaged in exploring other spiritual disciplines such as fasting, meditation, accountability groups and more.	Practices spiritual disciplines as a means of surrendering to Jesus and opening my life to the Holy Spirit's transforming activity.
	Fruit of the Spirit	Acknowledges that Christians such as me are given gifts by the Holy Spirit (Galatians 5:22)	Begins to incorporate and develop faith disciplines to grow the gifts of the spirit.	Fruits of the Spirit are known internally and demonstrated externally.	Continually grows in the inner qualities and outward actions identified as "the fruit of the Spirit" from Galatians 5:22.
	Small Groups	Sees some value of participating in Small Groups such as Bible Study & Sunday School.	Occasionally attend a small group or Sunday School class (2 out of 4 weeks) for personal growth.	Sharing my faith journey with others through small groups, mutual encouragement, and accountability as often as possible.	Shares my faith journey with a group of Christian friends in mutual encouragement, support, and accountability developing spiritual honesty and trust.

		Believing In Christ	Growing In Christ	Close To Christ	Christ-Centered
		First steps for those who desire to learn more about the Christian faith, the Church, and God.	*Believer growing in Christ primarily through large group experiences while developing a heart for the needs of others.*	*Spiritually mature disciple who desires a deeper level of shared discipleship with others and seeks ways to unselfishly serve.*	*Deeply committed disciple who surrenders to God, reproduces the Christian faith in the life of others, lives a life of service.*
SERVING GOD	Service To Others	Serves others when it is convenient.	Participates occasionally in a service project in the church or in the community.	I believe God calls me to be involved in the lives of the poor and suffering.	Is becoming an instrument of God's love in a broken, hurting world. Lives a life of service to others with a strong focus on the Bible's concern for the poor and for justice.
	Sharing Christ	Learning about the Good News but not comfortable sharing personal testimony of God's work in my life.	Developing my faith journey story and can share it with family and trusted friends.	Feels fully equipped to share my faith with non-Christians or nominal Christians. My behavior and actions reflect my faith.	Eager to share Christ's Good News in loving, winsome, and non-judgmental ways. Ready to "give an answer to anyone who asks the reason for your hope" 1 Peter 3:15
	Spiritual Gifts	Interested in taking a spiritual gifts assessment to learn how to serve others.	I know and occasionally use my spiritual gifts to fulfill God's purposes.	I regularly serve in ministry using my spiritual gifts.	Understands clearly which spiritual gifts and talents I have. Uses my gifts to bless others and build up the Body of Christ.
	Financial Gifts	Occasionally gives as the offering plate is passed or to a something special that interests me and my family.	I give as I feel I am able. I have a growing awareness of the need for God's direction in my finances, but struggle to balance it with my personal needs/wants.	Moving toward the tithe of my income. I know I need God's direction in my finances as he is the true source of all my blessings.	Tithing at least 10% of my income to the church, recognizing God owns everything, and submitting my financial life to God's guidance and control.
	Time	Being Active in Church and practicing my faith on a daily basis is important but a struggle to maintain	Making time for God and the practice of faith more of a priority in my life	Decisions on what projects, events, and activities in which I participate are weighed against how they best serve God.	I see time as a gift from God to be used in Keeping with God's Purpose, avoid compulsive business, and subject my calendar to God's guidance and control.

Regardless of what resources you use to develop your church's pathway, develop your system! Start today! Without an intentional faith development process in your church, we simply cannot expect or realize the God-sized IMPACT that each church has the potential to create. Everything flows from discipleship: leadership, evangelism, stewardship, worship design, mission, servanthood ... Without an intentional process to develop disciples of Jesus Christ in your church, we are simply not being the church in its full capacity and purpose. If you don't have one, create one so you can ensure the greatest potential for Kingdom IMPACT!

The Wesleyan Gift to the Church: Small Groups

The Sunday School Movement has served its purpose, and it is time for it to die. Well done, good and faithful ministry! One of the biggest points of confusion when beginning small groups for accountable discipleship is that the prevailing image of mainline Christian discipleship is the Christian Education model called Sunday School. The Sunday School was originally a literal school, a place to educate and provide literacy training for children during the Industrial Revolution. Because of the huge use of child labor during the 1800s, the only day children could learn to read (and therefore be able to read the Bible) was on Sunday. Even as compulsory schooling and public schools became the norm after 1870, the Sunday School Movement morphed in its mission but remained the central component of a church's Christian Education for children and adults. Note that title – "Christian Education" – the idea of discipleship is a much broader concept that impacts our entire relationship with

Christ and includes not only our minds but also our service, our witness, and our very souls. Discipleship is about a *relationship* with Christ, not just *knowing* things about Christ. I (Blake) was trained in seminary to lead Christian Education. However, education about doctrine and beliefs, while vitally important, cannot be the extent of our method for making disciples of Jesus Christ. Disciple-making is about accountability, opening our hearts, forming relationships, experiencing God's amazing grace together, and making a God-sized IMPACT in lives, communities, and the world. Wesley had it right in the 1700s: disciple-making requires small groups. I (Kay) attended the same Sunday School for 15 years as an adult before I had an amazing God moment in a short-term women's small group. I can honestly claim this is one of those 'moments in time' where I can name a huge step forward in my faith journey. While small groups can, of course, meet on Sunday morning at the church, small groups with a clear discipling purpose are one of God's ways of making an IMPACT in our very souls.

We have recently seen a rise in attention to Covenant Discipleship and in class meetings and band meetings, marks of our Wesleyan heritage.[19] By claiming this heritage, we are leapfrogging back in history to a time before the distractions of the Sunday School Movement and reconnecting to our Wesleyan and Methodist DNA of small group accountable discipleship. The genius of John Wesley's revival was that it did not end with the profession of faith

---

19 For more on Covenant Discipleship, see Steven W. Manskar's *Disciples Making Disciples: A Guide For Covenant Discipleship Groups And Class Leaders.* Nashville, Tennessee: Discipleship Resources, 2016. Professor Kevin Watson's recent works: *The Class Meeting : Reclaiming A Forgotten (And Essential) Small Group Experience.* Franklin, TN: Seedbed Publishing, 2013, and *The Band Meeting: Rediscovering Relational Discipleship in Transformational Community.* Franklin, TN: Seedbed Publishing, 2017.

in Christ's grace. Before Wesley left a town, lay leaders were put into place to guide others along the discipleship journey. Please note that organizational structure: the clergy equipped lay leaders and held them accountable for the management of the discipleship pathway. Early Methodism in England and America was a lay-led movement of IMPACTFUL and intentional discipleship. In the Eighteenth Century, no one waited on clergy to lead small groups to make disciples who nurtured and grew more disciples. In the 21st century, we can't wait to see what bible study the pastor wants to do this fall; the laity are called (and ordained by virtue of our baptisms) to make disciples and IMPACT the mission field today.

How this discipling work is enacted through the church should flourish from alignment with the congregation's unique vision and mission (see Chapter 7) and the intentional discipleship pathway (see above) that the pastor and board create to make a God-sized impact in souls and in the world.

When I (Blake) served a church early in my ministry, we agreed to a plan where small groups would become the basic building blocks of our discipleship formation. Worship attendance was up, and space was limited at this small blue-collar church, so it was easy for us to say, "Well, we are out of rooms, so perhaps we need to get creative and maximize our facility." A pilot group launched on Sunday night in a member's home, with the decision to rotate locations. New questions were asked about one another's souls instead of the laser focus on the latest curriculum from the denomination's publishing house.

To expand the program, small group leaders were trained by one of our key laity (she was the group leader for the pilot group and our future Small Group Coach) and me as the pastor. Groups started meeting on Sunday mornings and evenings – and weekday evenings as well. Most groups met weekly for an hour to 1.5 hours; one met two weeks on and one week off for 2 hours each time we gathered. Each group was required to have elements of knowing God by studying the Bible and Christian beliefs, loving God and others through mutual care and through sharing life together, and serving God and the community through missional work. My wife and I joined a new Wednesday night group of parents of young children led by our Administrative Board chairwoman. One young adult men's group met on Sunday night in the lobby of an auto maintenance shop owned by one of the members; the men's group utilized one of the unused car maintenance bays to build wheelchair ramps for seniors. Small group leaders all reported to the lay Small Group Coach, and she led regular semi-monthly gatherings of the small group leaders for mutual support, accountability, equipping, and adaptive problem-solving.

An updated adaption of the written monthly report each small group leader submitted to the lay Small Group Coach is included here so that you can see what was expected in the reporting relationship. Another version can be found online at VitalDisciples.org, a website created by the Arkansas Conference to resource church leaders.

MONTHLY SMALL GROUP CHECK-IN
Group Updates
Attendance Record:

Meeting Dates

	Date 1	Date 2	Date 3	Date 4	Date 5	Monthly Averages
Total # Attendance at Class Meetings						attendees
Regular Members						members
First Time Guests						guests
Regular Members Absent						absent

Has anyone joined your group over this past month? ❏ Yes ❏ No

Name / Phone Number	How / why they joined	Follow-Up
_____	_____	_____
_____	_____	_____
_____	_____	_____

Has anyone left your group over this past month? ❏ Yes ❏ No

Name / Phone Number	How / why they left	Follow-Up
_____	_____	_____
_____	_____	_____
_____	_____	_____

Activity Summary

Briefly share what the class/ accountability group did this month:

What transformation IMPACT are you seeing in and through the members of the group? (ie spiritual gifts, faith sharing, God-experiences, Impact in others)

Next Steps

What are your plans for the group for the next few months? How has your group intentionally discipled participants to be closer to Jesus Christ?

Just to Let You Know ...

Is there anything you'd like to celebrate? Do you have any concerns, prayer requests, or questions? (Note: For urgent concerns, please call the Small Group Coach / Pastor)

In creating this small group leader accountability system, our leadership team discovered a few things. First, real life is always messier than our plan. It took real work and buy-in to remain even somewhat consistent in our leadership accountability system, and in fact, the system did not survive the dual challenges of a change in pastors and the out-of-state move of the dedicated laywoman who served as our Small Group Coach. Second, I deeply underestimated the reactivity of some of the existing Sunday School classes during this transition. We invited (but certainly did not require) the existing Sunday School classes to become 'Wesleyan Small Groups' that happened to meet on Sunday mornings.

While we always said it was an option, some Sunday School leaders saw the growth and success of the small groups as a threat. Without the clear support of the lay leadership and constant contact with our district superintendent, the lay-led small group movement in that church would not have survived its first few months.

Lay-led small groups are our birthright as Wesleyan Christians! John Wesley believed that they were a means of grace, and we today see small groups as an instrument of Christ to make a God-sized IMPACT. While Wesley's language is of his era, the meaning and pattern of Wesleyan small groups is relevant as ever:

John Wesley's Rules for the Band-Societies
(drawn up Dec. 25, 1738)

The design of our meeting is, to obey that command of God, "Confess your faults one to another, and pray one for another, that ye may be healed." To this end, we intend,-

1. To meet once a week, at the least.

2. To come punctually at the hour appointed, without some extraordinary reason.

3. To begin (those of us who are present) exactly at the hour, with singing or prayer.

4. To speak each of us in order, freely and plainly, the true state of our souls, with the faults we have committed in thought, word, or deed, and the temptations we have felt, since our last meeting.

5. To end every meeting with prayer, suited to the state of each person present.

6. To desire some person among us; to speak his own state first, and then to ask the rest, in order, as many and as searching questions as may be, concerning their state, sins, and temptations.[20]

---

20 Wesley, John, "Rules of Band Societies, Drawn up December 25, 1738," in *The Works of John Wesley, Third Edition, Complete and Unabridged, Vol. VIII: Addresses, Essays, Letters,* ed. T. Jackson. London: Wesleyan Methodist Book Room, 1831, 1872. Reprinted: Grand Rapids: Baker Book House, 1978. Page 272.

Planning Your IMPACT

Questions for the Lay Leadership/Board Member

- Describe your church's discipleship process. Is it intentional? Is it effective? What, if any, changes need to be made to the process.

- How effective is your church's small group ministry? What adjustments need to be made?

- What are the discipleship expectations for leaders in your church?

Questions for the Disciple

- Describe where you are in your faith walk. What are next steps?

- How are you consistently moving closer to Christ in your daily walk?

Questions for the Pastor and Staff

- Describe your church's discipleship process. Is it intentional? Is it effective? What, if any, changes need to be made to the process.

- How effective is your church's small group ministry? What is the pastor's and staff's role in effecting change and in aligning the small group ministry to the church's overall discipleship pathway? What adjustments need to be made?

- How's the pastor and staff continuously encouraged in their own discipleship development?

Chapter Four

Relationships that make an IMPACT

During this time, as the disciples were increasing in numbers by leaps and bounds, hard feelings developed among the Greek-speaking believers – "Hellenists" – toward the Hebrew-speaking believers because their widows were being discriminated against in the daily food lines. So the Twelve called a meeting of the disciples. They said, "It wouldn't be right for us to abandon our responsibilities for preaching and teaching the Word of God to help with the care of the poor. So, friends, choose seven men from among you whom everyone trusts, men full of the Holy Spirit and good sense, and we'll assign them this task. Meanwhile, we'll stick to our assigned tasks of prayer and speaking God's Word."

The congregation thought this was a great idea. They went ahead and chose: Stephen, a man full of faith and the Holy Spirit, Philip, Procorus, Nicanor, Timon, Parmenas, Nicolas, a convert from Antioch.

Then they presented them to the apostles. Praying, the apostles laid on hands and commissioned them for their task. The Word of God prospered. The number of disciples in Jerusalem increased dramatically. Not least, a great many priests submitted themselves to the faith.

Acts 6:1-7 (The Message)

While this passage from the Acts of the Apostles shows us the first church argument, it also reminds us that relationships matter. The early church had gotten unbalanced in their relationships, and the whole endeavor was about to fail before it could begin. Missional relationships were being strained, and folks were feeling left out. The apostles were not managing their time for fruitful IMPACT. Once leadership expectations were modified, and the responsibility for maintaining and nurturing relationships was spread out amongst more leaders, the church was able to grow again.

Churches, we are in the relationship 'business.' Relationships are at the very core of all that we do. Building relationships is at the very core of who we are. Building relationships fulfills our mission of making disciples.

Let us unpack relationships a bit, as they pertain to the life of the congregation. The church is called to reach new people. We do that through building new relationships with new people. The church is called to *disciple*. As disciples, we are called to walk alongside others to help them grow in their discipleship. Ultimately, through all these relationships with others, we are all growing in our relationships with Jesus Christ. Church is ALL about relationships!

As central as relationships are to the vitality and potential impact of a church, the manner in which a faith community prioritizes and develops relationships can make them a tremendous asset or a stumbling block. If one were to study the life cycle of a church, you would find the church could be both growing or declining when relationships are a driving factor in the life of the church. How can that be? There are two factors which explain this. First, when a church is growing (the upside of the life cycle), there is a vision that is also driving the church. Vision is directing the church in the specific method in how God is calling the church to build relationships both internally and externally. Second, when relationships become a driving factor in a declining church, the church has become inwardly focused on relationships between members of the congregation – fellowship. They have lost focus on reaching new people.

Somewhere along the way, we have come to believe that pastors are mostly (if not solely) responsible for making disciples. Pastors are to lead the church. Pastors are to equip the laity. The laity are called to build the relationships. The laity's dependence on the pastor for building relationships with new people has led to our churches decline. The pastors' lack of equipping the laity has led to our churches decline. We are all responsible! Yet, now that we know better, we can do better.

Furthermore, when new relationships are all formed directly with the pastor and not with others in the congregation, the pastor's relational capacity is soon reached. It is incredibly difficult for one person to have more than 75-80 personal relationships. This phenomenon is clearly connected to the average church size being 75 people in the United States.[21] We limit the size of our church and its potential IMPACT to reach new people when relationship building is left solely up to the pastor. In addition, if people are only connected relationally to the pastor, the person will likely leave the church if the pastor leaves the church. Bottom line, folks: relationship-building is the responsibility of the congregation!

Building relationships in the life of the church is

---

21 The Hartford Institute for Religion Research is an extension of Hartford Seminary and the scholars of the HIRR study religious groups and organizations. See http://hirr.hartsem.edu/research/fastfacts/fast_facts.html.

multi-faceted. It starts with the vision and desire to reach new people, followed by hospitality, connections, discipleship, fellowship, worship, ministries, and congregational care. Each part of the life of the church is about relationships. A church with relational impact is a church that sees each ministry through the lens of relationship building. Let's look at each of these areas a bit closer.

Hospitality

Think of hospitality as a first impression. We have all heard it said that you do not have a second chance to make a first impression. This is so true in the life of the church. But where do those first impressions occur in the church? We often are misled to believe the first impression is at the door of the sanctuary or perhaps the front door. We would challenge you that hospitality begins much sooner. Most likely, hospitality begins online. Yes, online! What kind of first impression would a guest receive from your church's Facebook page? Your website? Are there stories of transformation and relationships, or simply pictures of an empty building? Most often social media is used for insider communication without much consideration for a new person. Have someone not affiliated with your church take a look at your online presence and give you some feedback.

Next, we want to think about hospitality as someone approaches your church's location. Is there directional signage to find the church, where to park, and what entrance to use? Is the guest being greeted in the parking lot, at the exterior entrance door, and at the sanctuary door? Is the interior signage adequate for a guest to find their way easily around the facility, paying special attention to signage for restrooms, children's ministries, and the worship area?

Is the bulletin guest-friendly, or are we using insider or churchy language and acronyms? Is there a congregation-al-wide culture of hospitality, or is hospitality left up to the greeting team alone?

How about worship? Is worship designed to encourage new people to be comfortable and encounter Christ, or is it designed totally for the sake of those already in the church? Think about announcements; is the content and delivery guest-friendly? Could a guest feel invited and easily figure out how to step into ministry and the congregation's web of relation-ships? Are our pastoral prayers filled with references to Hazel's surgery outcome and Bob's grief while members nod in know-ing agreement, and guests are left perplexed and mildly embar-rassed by the sharing of private information? Do we forget we have guests among us once the benediction concludes and rush out the door, or do we intentionally offer an opportunity for the forming of new relationships after worship?

Often we mistake friendliness for hospitality. It is rare that we, the authors, encounter a church who is not friendly, or at least polite. However, it is often that we encounter a church that is friendly but fails to offer opportunities to form relationships. People can go most anywhere to find friendliness, but most people are looking for something far beyond friendly. They are looking for relationships. They are looking for a place to belong.

We must also think about our building as it relates to hospitality. Churches often allow outside groups to use the building. The imagined hope is that if someone enters the building for another activity, they will somehow find their way to the life of the congregation, most often through worship. Yet we offer no intentional pathway for this to occur. Instead, we have the crazy idea that some Sunday morning, the person who goes to scouts on Thursday night will wake up and suddenly decide to go to church on Sunday. Friends, this rarely occurs, if at all. How does your church offer hospitality to the groups using the building so that there is an opportunity to build relationships? If a church is not willing to offer hospitality and opportunities for relationship building, then, with all due respect, we must ask, why are you doing it? Issuing a key is not hospitality. Churches are not in the landlord business. We are in the people business. If you are not willing to invest in the people using the building, then we must ask ourselves why outsiders are using the building.

If your church would like to strengthen your IMPACT through hospitality, we recommend *Clip In* by Ozier & Haworth or Chapter Two of Kay's *Gear Up*.

Fellowship

Fellowship is a good thing. Or, it can be a good thing. Yet many churches allow it to trump everything else. We sometimes mistake fellowship for hospitality. Fellowship is inwardly focused – relationships with the existing friends within the congregation. Fellowship is part of our small group experience – doing life together. Fellowship is less about Sunday mornings. If your worship is on Sunday mornings, then Sunday morning should be more about preparing for and having the expectation to receive guests. If we are too busy with fellowship, we will miss the opportunity to be hospitable and build a relationship with a new person. Hospitality is outwardly focused.

Take a look at the life of your congregation. Is your

calendar full of activities for those who are already part of the church? Or does your church offer a variety of activities for both new people as well as existing people?

Bottom line is that a church needs both fellowship and hospitality. Just make sure we are concentrating on the right piece of relationships at the appropriate time!

Connections

going on to perfection

Connections Ministry is the black hole between a first-time guest and a person entering into a discipling process. In our role as congregational consultants, most churches we have encountered do not have an intentional process to connect a first-time guest to Christ and others and move that person through a growth process toward becoming a mature disciple. One foot planted in worship a time or two a month can easily move right on out the door. But one foot planted firmly in worship AND the other foot firmly planted into the life of the congregation through a small group, mission group, or serving as a volunteer is much more likely to stay planted and eventually bear fruit.

prayer partners

Connection is a one-on-one relational journey where a disciple walks alongside a new person to help them find their connection in the life of the congregation. This could be done by a pastor, but it really should be considered to be part of a lay ministry. The pastor can organize, equip, and help the connections ministry, but there is a special quality of connection and depth created when a deeply-committed Christ follower disciples another person. There are a few reasons for this: First, relationships in a church should look more like a spider web rather than spokes on a wheel all leading to the pastor. A pastor-centric connections ministry

65

will not build up your church toward the web of lay relationships that are required for a healthy and IMPACTFUL congregation. Second, it sets up horrible pastoral expectations in that the guests you are acculturating get the message that the pastor is supposed to take care of all their relational needs in the church. A lay-centered connections ministry speaks to the value of the laity and demonstrates from the very beginning how disciples are supposed to serve and lead. Third, pastors change, and when pastors leave churches that are relationally pastor-centric, the congregation is left looking at each other as functional strangers. Sometimes, it could even mean that everyone whose relationship with the congregation was through the pastor also leaves the church, either following the pastor to a new church in town or drifting away in search of a new pastor with whom they can be in relationship.

The difficulty of building an intentional connections system in a church often is rooted in the fact that folks do not arrive in the church narthex as empty containers waiting to be filled up with our church program and doctrine. Today, there is little cultural expectation or advantage in joining a church. When people show up, there is a *reason*. It might be a search for meaning, a recent loss, a private pain, a sense of guilt, an unfulfilled hope, or simply an urging of the Holy Spirit. Some walk through our doors having grown up in a church community and having attended worship their whole lives; others have never heard the Good News. Some are babes in the faith, and some may be mature Christ-centered disciples. And of course, a few may believe and strongly affirm that they are mature disciples while it is evident to everyone but themselves that the sanctifying grace of God still has a fair bit of work ahead. People are messy, and our connections systems must be flexible enough to meet people where they are as unique children of God.[22] Perhaps we can learn a bit from recovery ministries here; the efficacy of 12-Step programs depends on sponsors who are dedicated to walking alongside new arrivals and connecting them to the group. What might a sponsor program look like in your congregation? As you build your system, keep an eye on your church's back door, tracking those who never seem to join a small group or whose attendance in worship begins to get spotty. Figure out what is 'sticky' in your system versus the ministries or worship services that never seem to build traction with new folks. What you discover will help you immensely as you build a connections ministry that can have real IMPACT on people's lives. The era of 'church shopping' is over – your church may be the last chance a person will give to *any* church. We need to get this right for the sake of the Kingdom! For more information on connections and how to set up a connections process, please see Chapter Three of Kay's book *Gear Up*. Regardless of the system you create, we need to be patient but intentional. Ultimately, connections ministry is helping another soul discover Jesus Christ through the life of the church and its ministries.

Discipling In Relationship

Chapter Three described the intentional disciple-making process that can truly make an impact on lives and the world. The mission of the church is to make disciples of Jesus Christ for the transformation of the world (Matthew 28). Most all of

---

22 Actually, both our connections systems and our intentional discipling pathways must be designed to be flexible, meeting people where they are and honoring the spiritual journey that they have already taken.

us inherently know this. Yet most churches are struggling with 'how' to do this. We often are misled to believe that disciples are made by simply attending church. Maybe we attend church AND go to Sunday school or small group. But have we as the church really examined what is taking place in worship and small groups (Sunday school included)? Do we have an intentional plan of helping people grow closer in relationship with Jesus Christ? While we earlier examined the intentional discipling pathways, disciples are not built in a factory; they are formed in and through relationships that make an impact.

Too often we think about small groups as a place for people to connect. Yes, that is true. But let's challenge ourselves to think about that connection a bit deeper. First, what is the goal of the small group? Have we really articulated it? Do we equip those leading? Do we have resources? Do we have a pathway for them to follow? Discipling is about doing life with other Christians as we grow closer to Jesus – in loving, understanding, and becoming more Christ-like. All of this is best done in community. But what does this really mean? In short, doing life together is about being real with one another. It is about revealing your true self in order to find your authentic self in Christ. As a church, how are you equipping your small group leaders to lead others in this authentic relationship? Are we really willing to walk alongside people in an intentional pathway to grow closer to God?

Mature disciples disciple others. Mature disciples do not wait to be fed spiritually. Instead, mature disciples understand and have a desire to feed others literally and figuratively. Intentional discipling/faith development leads people to do evangelism as part of their discipleship practices – their faithfulness (building relationships with others outside the church). Is your church full of people who understand this basic principle of being a mature disciple? If not, what will your church do to create a culture and understanding of growing disciples who grow new disciples? How can we move our churches from a consumer mentality to a discipleship multiplication mentality?

Relational Worship

Worship is relational. Worship is the opportunity to experience God and to grow in your relationship with God. Worship is about praising God. Worship is intended to be IMPACTFUL! Is your church creatively creating worship to be relational? Relational to God? Relational to new people? If so, praise God! If not, what steps are you willing to take as a congregation to move in that direction?

Too often pastors plan worship in a silo. Not only is this a sure way to become stagnant, but it is a lost opportunity to allow people to serve. Many lay people are passionate about worship and have great gifts to offer. Putting a group of people together to design worship is what we refer to as a Worship Design Team. Not only is a Worship Design Team a space to collaboratively create a 'wow' worship experience for all, but it is a great use of spiritual gifts and a tremendous relationship-building opportunity. Chapter Six will focus specifically on "Impactful Worship," but in this chapter, suffice it say that if those designing and leading worship are not in relationship with one another, how could we ever imagine that the congregation will be able to connect in relationship with God or each other?

In our experience, when the laity are brought into worship design, worship is taken to a whole new level.

Creativity abounds, and more people are invested in worship and bringing the best the church has to offer through worship.

Congregational worship is also a place to encourage relationships that make an IMPACT in each other's lives. I (Blake) spent most of my adult life as a preacher behind the pulpit, so I was stunned when I moved to work in our conference office and began visiting different churches. I could visit a church and never have a conversation that I didn't initiate. It took me a while to understand, but I drew upon my work as a lifeguard when I was a teenager for the closest example. One of the things lifeguards learn is that there is a 'bystander effect' in an emergency – the larger a crowd, the less likely anyone is going to take action. The only way to break the effect is through training or assigned responsibility. I found that there is a strong bystander effect in place on Sunday mornings. The responsibility to initiate contact is so diffused amongst the congregation no one takes action. One helpful training tool is found in Jim Ozier's book, *Clip In: Risking Hospitality in Your Church*. Ozier advocates congregational training in the '5-10-Link' rule[23]: using the five minutes before and after worship to relate to guests, connecting to anyone you don't know who crosses within 10 feet of your location, and linking guests to other members to build up community. This hospitality training is an excellent start and can break the bystander effect that keeps members from engaging with guests. An additional approach to interrupt the bystander effect is to build responsibility. We know, and often bemoan, that regular worship attenders often sit in the same seat week after week. What would happen if you made

23 Ozier, Jim. Clip In: Risking Hospitality In Your Church. Nashville, TN: Abingdon Press, 2014, pp. 27–30.

this an asset? Select and equip regular worship attenders with a gregarious spirit to become 'pew section shepherds' who are responsible for knowing those in their section of the sanctuary. They can keep an eye out for when a family has been missing for a few weeks and be the first to welcome worship guests that sit in their zone of responsibility. Serving as a pew section shepherd is an awesome way to build rapport with members and guests and create opportunities for IMPACTFUL relationships among the worshiping community.

Ministries

What is the purpose of a church having ministries? Ministries provide the opportunities for the church to realize its mission of making disciples for the transformation of the world. Ministries are the strategies for the mission and vision (God's preferred future for the church to uniquely make disciples) of your church. Ministries should not be carried out simply for the sake of history. Nor should ministries or programs be ends unto themselves. Rather, ministries are the unique method in which the church offers for people to grow in their discipleship and IMPACT the world for the Glory of God.

Ministry is where individuals within the church have the opportunity to use their gifts to serve God through the church. Too often we fill positions with people rather than fit people into places to use their giftedness. Ministry is about the people serving with people. All are called to ministry – not just clergy. How we engage in ministry may change in the different seasons of life, but we firmly believe that your call into ministry never expires until you do. Without

71

everyone in the congregation sharing their unique spiritual gifts, the congregation will not be as vital as it could be when everyone is giving of their gifts. How do we engage with people inside our congregation to help them discover their gifts and help them find a way to use them?

Congregational Care

In the midst of the eternal 'to-do' list for a church, there are also some functions that really belong on the 'to-BE' list. A community of excellent congregational care is chief on the list of what a congregation 'should be.' In the first few centuries of the church's existence, even a fierce pagan persecutor of the faith had to admit, "Behold how these Christians love one another!" Even in antiquity, people saw that great congregational care makes an impact on people's lives and their communities! Caring for our congregation is part of our being in relationship with one another – part of being the body of Christ. Yet many times this is a stumbling block for our churches. Congregations sometimes expect *pastoral* care rather than *congregational* care. Pastoral care is done exclusively by the pastor. Congregational care is done by the congregation as part of our responsibility to one another as fellow believers. There are critical times when pastoral care is appropriate, but most times, congregational care is best done by the laity. However, we often do not adequately equip our people who have the spiritual gifts of caregiving.

In addition, we have become clergy-dependent with a false expectation that all care should come directly from the pastor. This expectation not only limits a church's growth, but it also robs us, the laity, of the ministry of caring that is part of Christ's calling on our lives. This is a critical part of ministry that is a calling of the laity. Reclaim it! Do not allow the pastor to steal your ministry!

When I (Blake) was moved from an associate pastor position in a mid-sized congregation in a city and assigned to be the solo pastor of a small congregation in Arkansas, I learned an awesome lesson in my first few weeks at my new congregation. While I was still trying to get my bearings, I received a phone call that eventually made a huge impact not only on my own ministry but also on the entire congregation.

A member, Liz, called during my first week, asking if I would be willing to take communion to her elderly mother in the nursing home every week. Her mother was a member of the larger 'First Church' in town, but she thought it would be nice if I visited every week as well. In an effort to be transparent, I said that I wasn't sure about the time demands in this new position, and I needed some time to figure out the right balance for pastoral care and the other parts of ministry, so I couldn't commit to a weekly visit. However, if she would like to schedule a visit now and then and go with me to visit her mom, I would be happy to celebrate communion with them. The 'no ... but ...' answer seemed to satisfy Liz, and I thought it balanced my pastoral role with Liz while not crossing the boundaries with the pastors and staff of the First Church. But the Holy Spirit was working in the background, and Liz called a few weeks later, wondering if there was some way to train a team of laity to visit the sick and homebound. Liz and I ended up creating a congregational care system with a team of trained lay chaplains that she scheduled every week.

Liz and I crafted a curriculum and resource book, a process for reporting, and a covenant for all the caregivers.

We commissioned them in worship, and they set to work, expanding the congregation's vision for congregational care, and every lay chaplain deployed has impacted dozens of lives over the years while experiencing the impact on their own lives by living out their calling. Meanwhile, I never stopped visiting the homebound and sick (in rural Arkansas, a pastor who does not visit better start packing), but I did use the majority of my relational time focusing on critical care issues, leadership development, and guests.

Looking back, I realize that my own willingness to please came very close to robbing my new congregation of experiencing God's calling and making a true IMPACT in the church and community. If I had simply said 'yes' to Liz's first request, Liz would have never experienced the joy of leading an amazing cohort of lay chaplains, I would not have had the opportunity to focus my leadership energy on making new disciples, and the laity of the congregation would never have had the experience of caring and receiving Christ-centered care from each other. But instead of robbing ministry from the laity, at a critical moment, I gave it away, and the members of the congregation were able to live out their calling more fully by walking alongside each other during times of difficulty. Along the way, I discovered that equipping and leading the laity in intentional relationship-building and congregational care enabled the church to grow larger while actually becoming more intimate.

Connectional Relationships

Both of us (Kay and Blake) currently serve out of annual conference (regional judicatory) offices in different regions of the United States. In a time of institutional distrust, organizational uncertainty, and divisive denominational politics, it is not a surprise to either of us that some congregational leaders can be a bit wary when we roll into the church parking lot, saying, "We are from the bishop's office, and we are here to help." We have realized, however, that most laypeople are excited to get resources from the denomination to strengthen their IMPACT in their community. We believe that the key part in denominational relationships is the 'relationship' part! If your church only relates to the district superintendent, conference office, or bishop when there is an existential conflict or an anger-infused problem, then naturally any contact with the larger denomination will create anxiety on everyone's part.

This anxiety is probably why denominational and judicatory communication from the district or conferences offices seem to stop at the pastor's office inbox. As two resource people devoted to equipping and growing local churches, we have seen a tremendous hunger among the laity for resources, new ideas, and assistance from the larger denomination. Whether it is caused by the fullness of a congregation's internal calendar or outright mistrust on the part of the pastor, both of us have been surprised and frustrated by how denominational information and opportunities are blocked from ever getting to the laity.

There is an alternative way! Treat the people in your denominational structures and in your fellow congregations as opportunities for IMPACTFUL relationships. We, the laity, need to get proactive! Check your conference's website and the website of denominational offices. You may find everything from curriculum, free or inexpensive communication tools, leadership equipping, and access to demographic and statistical information. There may even be grant applications for new ministries. Search online, call around, and most importantly, take initiative! You may well discover amazing resources and occasions for partnerships that increase your IMPACT. You will also have an IMPACT on other congregations and maybe even the larger work of the church. Most denominational structures and committees are in dire need of Christ-centered laity to help guide everything from where new churches will be planted to who will be ordained. We have heard from countless lay leaders who have said that serving in these denominational structures has broadened their perspective and increased the IMPACT of their home churches. We are in mission together, and we need one another – that's what it means to be a connectional church!

Community Networks And Partnerships

Our next chapter will focus on missions that make an impact, particularly creating missions that are intentional about sharing Christ and sharing our lives in relationships. But before your church can really have an IMPACT on missional outreach (building relationships with those you are serving alongside), you must first be in relationship with your larger community. After finding out that neighborhood relationships had broken down over the years in their community, Colorado church leaders Jay Pathak and Dave Runyon began with a question: "What if Jesus meant that we should love our actual neighbors?" In response, they wrote a book and began a movement called the 'Art of Neighboring'[24] to equip and encourage the laity to engage their actual

---

24 For more information on the art of neighboring, read Pathak, Jay, and Dave Runyon. *The Art Of Neighboring: Building Genuine Relationships Right Outside Your Door*. Grand Rapids, MI: Baker Books, 2012. You can also visit http://www.artofneighboring.com/ for a whole host of tools and resources.

neighborhoods block by block. Churches across the country have grabbed hold of this idea and are supporting movements in their congregations to shift some of their relational energy outward into their local communities rather than only inward to support the church's program.

I (Blake) made a few tweaks to this 'Art of Neighboring' concept. Living in the mostly rural state of Arkansas, mapping the people and relationships in neighborhoods and blocks can be a foreign concept, so I have broadened the idea to encourage church leadership teams to map their relational networks – networks such as motorcycle riding clubs, card playing circles, civic groups, cattle auctions, professional organizations, and community theatre – and encourage the laity to use these opportunities for networking for Jesus Christ.

Witnessing doesn't have to be heavy-handed. It could be as simple as sharing the IMPACT your church has had in your own life and recommending your church when others are going through the similar moments in their lives. Several years ago, the United Methodist Church had a training program to market the church. Part of the training included witnessing to FRAN – Friends, Relatives, Acquaintances, Neighbors. While this acronym is getting a bit old and dusty, the truth is that we still aren't doing it! Imagine the IMPACT of every layperson looking at their networks and local neighborhoods as opportunities to bless others!

Conclusion

Friends, relationships take time. Relationships are messy. Yet living in community together is really what church life is all about. As Christians, we are called to be in relationship with others to deepen our own faith, share our stories with others so that they might come to know Christ, and walk alongside others so that they deepen their relationship with Christ. To be the IMPACTFUL church, we must be willing to invest in relationships inside the church and even more importantly with our neighbors!

Planning Your IMPACT

Questions for the Lay Leadership/Board Member

- How impactful are relationships in your church on a scale of 1-10 (1 - not at all impactful, and 10 - super impactful)? Share your answers with the rest of the team. Discuss your various rankings.

- What area of relationships does the church do the best? Challenged by the most? Share your answers with the team.

- Name one area of relationships your church will work on in the coming year. How will the church become more impactful in that area?

Questions for the Disciple

- How are you forming relationships with people you do not know?

78

- How is your relationship with Christ? How are you specifically growing in your faith? How are you helping others grow in their faith?

- How are you walking alongside others during times of difficulty?

- Who specifically will you be discipling in the upcoming year?

Questions for the Pastor & Staff

- What relationships are you carrying in your church that would be best carried by the laity?

  Everything

- Is each staff person serving in their area of relational giftedness? What shifts need to be made if any?

- How are you intentionally equipping your congregation with IMPACTFUL relationships?

Chapter Five

Missions That Make
An IMPACT

'I'm telling the solemn truth: Whenever you did one of these things to someone overlooked or ignored, that was me – you did it to me.'

Matthew 25:40 (The Message)

As a church and as a Christian people, we are called to do good deeds for people. It is who we are and what is expected of us as a Christ-follower. After all, we are called to transform the world. This world transformation comes partially by being Christ-like in our world to feed the hungry, provide drink to the thirsty, cloth the naked, and visit the sick and imprisoned. This is the sort of people God called us to be and what is expected of us.

Nevertheless, there are a couple of places where we consistently find churches struggling with IMPACTFUL missions. Churches often do mission work, but they fail to have missions with IMPACT! First, we have often become passive in our missions. In other words, we have become good check writers and provide great "stuff" for people in need (school supplies, sock, mittens, coats, blankets, clean-up kits). We have become more like a charity and other secular organizations. Secondly, we often leave the work of missions to a selected group - the few, the proud, the mission's committee/team. When mission is left up to the committee, often times it leaves 90% of the congregation disconnected from the mission and thus the majority of the congregation is disconnected from ministry beyond the walls of the church. We are using only a fraction of the potential God has given us, and we miss an opportunity for IMPACT in our community and world.

Face to Face Missions Impact!

Many churches are doing some really good mission projects. Yet, we are missing a great opportunity to "see" and build relationships with the people with whom we are in ministry. I (Kay) refer to this as active missions rather than the passive missions mentioned above. It is an opportunity to be "face to face" with people. When we are fully present with the people with whom we are in ministry, we can have experiential and relational IMPACT! A fruitful, Christ-centered, and grace-filled outreach ministry is not really about what we do "to" or "for" people. Rather, it is how we build relationships with people.

When we leave relationships out of missions, we are leaving out the best potential for true IMPACT. IMPACTFUL missions are grounded in authentic relationships. They are no longer about the anonymous giving of stuff. When two or more are gathered, Christ is with you. Relational missions provides opportunity for the Holy Spirit to do its thing - IMPACT souls! Missions without relationship reduces the opportunity for "Holy Moments."

When I (Blake) accompanied a church youth group to visit Canvas Community, a downtown United Methodist missional church based in a storefront, to prepare and share a meal with the congregation and its homeless neighbors, we discovered the simultaneous joy and fear that goes along with ministry *with* instead of *to*. For instance, there were more youth than "jobs" preparing and serving the food, so Paul Atkins, the ordained deacon at the church, was thrilled, "Great, so the rest of you do the important thing – visit with our neighbors!" I and the youth were blessed to have some great conversations , see some artwork that one of the congregation's friends had been painting, and hear stories of God's blessings – even testimonies of God's salvation work – among the neighbors who considered the church a safe place and a spiritual home where they had met Jesus through relationships.

As we seek to move from missions *for* "those people" to relational missions, we move from doing "charity work" to authentic missional engagement *with* people and *with* our community. We begin to acknowledge the souls of others beyond our walls, and we seek to connect at a soul level with relational ministries of justice and compassion. We become an outwardly-focused church that is engaged in their community, meeting needs and building relationships with the unchurched. We take responsibility for those needs and for the souls who do not yet know Christ.

Knowing Your Mission Field

It is essential to know your mission field. But before then, you must name your mission field. Often church leaders and pastors use a generic surrounding area to the church to learn about the community. The generic area might include the whole town, a few miles radius of the church, a zip code, a school district, a neighborhood, etc. These areas may indeed be the mission field for the church. But allow us to challenge you a bit on this. Has your church intentionally studied and prayed over the area to determine what area God is calling you to reach? Without prayerful discernment along with intentional and strategic research, we are simply throwing a dart on the map. Or maybe, we fail to even throw the dart, possibly in a desire to "connect to everyone." But let's be realistic: "everyone" is not attending your church now, *everyone* never has attended your church, and our natural desire to include and invite *everyone* has meant that most of our churches are shrinking. Our desire to include *everyone* has meant that *no one* is being newly connected and impacted by your congregation.

Without a clear and intentional "ownership" of the neighborhood or slice of the community the church is called to reach, there is no way the church can fully know the needs of the mission field and build relationships within the mission field. Instead, it is what we "think" we know rather than "knowing" what we know. Rev. Joseph Daniels, author of *Walking with Nehemiah: Your Community Is Your Congregation,*[25] served simultaneously as the Lead Pastor of Emory United Methodist Church in Washington, D.C., and as a Superintendent of the Greater Washington District in the Baltimore Washington Conference. During his time on the cabinet, he encouraged the clergy and lay leaders of the churches in his district to claim their ZIP codes for Jesus Christ. The "ZIP" in ZIP code is an acronym referring to Zone Improvement Plan. Since 1963, the postal service began an improvement plan to use the five digit ZIP code to sort and deliver mail more efficiently. Rev. Daniels charge was for every church to have a Zone Improvement Plan for claiming Christ in their neighborhood.

Determining the mission field usually has little to do with where the current worship attendees live because many churches have become drive-in churches. That is, regular attenders might have lived in the neighborhood at one time, but have since moved outside the church's neighborhood. When churches have a great number of worship attenders no longer living in the neighborhood, we have often lost touch with our neighborhood. We are working under decades of old information and assuming our old understandings and beliefs are true of today's neighborhood, too. Too often the neighborhood changes, but the church simply is not keeping up. We become irrelevant to our neighbors. We lose touch, making it even more difficult in today's world to reach new people in our mission field. After a while, the topic of the

---

25 Daniels, Joseph W. *Walking With Nehemiah: Your Community Is Your Congregation.* Nashville: Abingdon Press, 2014.

neighborhood stops coming up in meetings because no one at the table has any personal investment in the church's mission field. I (Blake) know of one church that found it more comfortable to have an "everyone is invited" cookout across town in a hidden park rather than use the church campus or a nearby park down the street from the local elementary school.

Laity must be the local experts of their community. In our tribe (United Methodist Church), pastors are moved from church to church, often every few years. This makes it even more important for lay leaders to intimately know the mission field. Anytime our neighborhood changes, it should change the makeup of the church. The church should ebb, flow and journey alongside the neighborhood. We must be intimately aware of the current demographics and trends.

When we are discerning our mission field and aligning our vision to it, there are some questions that church leaders might wrestle with such as:

- *Who are we as a congregation now?* Where do our members live? What are our social and professional networks? What partnerships do we have with local groups and institutions?

- *Who is our neighbor?* Describe in detail their age, socio-economics, jobs, children, worries, struggles, dreams, etc.

- *What is the gap between our congregation and our mission field?* How do our notions of the community track against statistics and demographic information?

- *What must we do, give up, and/or change to reach our neighbors for Christ?*

"With" and "of" the Community

I (Kay) had the great privilege of working with the Hamilton United Methodist Church in Hamilton, Missouri. The town of Hamilton is a small, rural town in the north central part of the state with a population of about 1700 and the church worshipers are around 160. Although it is a smaller town, the church has a huge community IMPACT! This church has "adopted" the town. For example, when the school refers to "the church," they are referring to the United Methodist Church. The school sees the church as a vital part of the community. They are partners in supporting children and their families in the community.

The church provides gift certificates to their clothing closet for the nurses and counselors at the school to give out as needed to students. The church hosts the back-to-school teacher luncheon in the church building providing not only a meal, but also hospitality, relationships and even the offer of being a prayer partner for the teachers who desire to have one. The church is a vital part of the heartbeat of this town and has integrated the life of the church into the life of the citizens. This is community IMPACT at its best.

We don't have to go on this journey alone. In today's world, most congregations simply don't have the resources to be the transformation agent God needs if we insist on acting as independent entities. Creative partnerships can maximize our potential IMPACT by expanding our reach, bridging cultures to vulnerable populations, and creating an economy of scale. In the gospels, a few fish and some bread are brought to Jesus, and from this simple meal, thousands are fed. God can work miracles in the presence of the multitudes!

For churches that have not partnered with others

recently, a good starting place is always the local public school. Folks care about children, and today's schools could always use our help. It might start with a simple conversation with the principal, some snacks in the teacher's lounge, and providing crayons and pencils for the student supply closet. It could develop into backpack feeding programs, caring for the playground equipment, coat drives, sponsorship of the PTA, reading mentors, and weekly homework tutors.

Most planning meetings about missions get stuck when we look at our resources and then at the enormity of a problem in our community. What we often forget is that an abundance of resources, knowledge, and skills exists outside of our church. So when we are planning our missional IMPACT, we should consider how other local churches, hospitals, schools and universities, non-profits, government agencies, and even local businesses might be able to partner together.

It may be that a local organization is already doing a particular specialized ministry and they are making a huge impact. Instead of recreating the wheel, why not provide resources and people-power to build up the Kingdom through a partnership?

In the last chapter, we wrote about networks. What would happen if congregation members involved with civic organizations and local nonprofits gathered to share what they have been seeing through these organizations, perhaps in a set of conversations led by your board or your mission's committee. Start the meeting with your church's mission and vision to frame the discussion (we are not embarrassed that the church is not about doing "nice things", but is about making disciples of Jesus Christ to transform the world), but then let the conversation flow, celebrating what

God is already doing in your community through each of these members. A few hours together in conversation could quickly evolve into a year's worth of partnership opportunities that would help your church transform your corner of God's world! Along the way, you would also be strengthening the relational bonds of your community, empower laity throughout your church, and help folks in your community know that your church seeks to be outwardly-focused.

Creating a Third Place

A term has gained traction in social sciences and marketing: the concept of the "Third Place." The idea is that communities need third places beyond work/school and home to build up relationships and social engagement. These third places could be coffee shops, bookstores, hobby groups, sports leagues, and (of course) churches. The decline of third places is described in Robert Putnam's 2000 book *Bowling Alone: The Collapse and Revival of American Community.*[26]

In the years since that book was written, we have seen alternative ways that folks have sought to create 21st century third places, from robust online communities to local libraries; attempting to refashion themselves with engaging and inviting classes like "Adulting 101" for millennials. Congregations seeking to be fruitful and IMPACTFUL will need to figure out how to not only reach out beyond its walls to engage the community, but also use their existing facilities to create healthy and inviting third places to bless the neighborhood. So, don't get stuck on the word "place" and imagine it as only being your facility. Being a "third

---

26 Putnam, Robert D. *Bowling Alone: The Collapse And Revival Of American Community.* New York: Simon & Schuster, 2000.

place" isn't so much about the *place*, it's about the relationships. No one will listen to the Good News of Jesus Christ on
our lips if our actions are already yelling that we could care
less about our neighborhood.

Some churches are willing to re-imagine themselves to
make an IMPACT in their community. St. Andrew United
Methodist Church in Metro Little Rock is a very small church
that most folks would have written off as about to close its
doors. But the members and clergy team (a retired African
American elder and a retired Anglo deacon who is trained in
Hispanic ministry) decided to try anything to connect to their
community. It was difficult.

The community's demographics had transitioned from
working-class white to black to Hispanic quite quickly within
thirty years, poverty and its related challenges had risen
considerably in the neighborhood, and the church had not
been able to stay connected to its community. The building was much larger than the small congregation needed.
The church decided to reconnect to its community. They
had assets that could bless the neighborhood. They invited
community agencies and municipal offices that interact with
citizens to be housed in the empty classrooms of the church
for a minimal rent.

They started ESL classes and did ServSafe food handling
certification training in English and Spanish using the
church's kitchen so that people could more easily get jobs in
restaurants. Sewing classes and groups that combined prayer
and devotion with skills training helped recent immigrants
start cottage businesses. Folks from the church visited every
commercial business and trailer park, asking for nothing
but offering prayer at every stop. The church is still small,

but their IMPACT is huge! The church has even teamed up with the conference's Center for Vitality to offer workshops for other churches across Arkansas to strategize how to connect with local partners, engage their neighborhood relationally and missionally, and IMPACT their own communities. Of course, not every church facility is designed or located to do a "third place" ministry well. That is why some churches are engaging in relational ministries outside of their buildings, with ideas like coffee shop ministries and summer worship in a local park followed by free community picnics.

I (Kay) recently had a pastor inquire about the concern of the school creating a new bus stop in front of the church. Instead of seeing this as a perfect opportunity to bless the children routinely and build relationships, the first concern was of liability and possible damage. First let me share that the bus stop was a public sidewalk. Secondly, my heart breaks to see liability and potential damage as our first reaction. Imagine hanging out on that sidewalk with the children and possibly even some parents could get to know them and build relationships. Could we offer warm beverages on cold days or umbrellas on rainy days?

The Shift

To have a Mission with IMPACT, most congregations will find the need for a real shift. This is a shift into a more "holistic" approach of good deeds. It is less about writing checks and sending stuff across town (and across the country) and more about how are we in relational ministry with our neighbors. Congregations who engage in missions with IMPACT are one with their community.

91

These vital congregations reflect their neighborhoods. They constantly challenge themselves with questions of how the church can be a wider community of grace to impact lives, the larger community, and perhaps even the greater world.

Any organization can do charity work. And many excellent organizations do wonderful and essential charity. What differentiates the church from other charity or social groups is that we are in the Jesus business. All we need is to be led back to the purpose for which the church exists - to make disciples of Jesus Christ for the transformation of the world. In order to live out this purpose, we must be in relationship with the people we are doing ministry within our community. Churches with mission IMPACT get this and do this!

Planning Your IMPACT

Questions for the Lay Leadership/Board Member

- Describe your mission's field. How was the mission's field identified?

- What type of mission work is the church currently involved in? What shift, if any, would need to be made to have relational missions? How might your church facility become a "third place" to build up relationships in your larger community?

- How well do you know your community? What do you need to learn about your community? With whom might you partner to make an IMPACT?

Questions for the Disciple

- Describe the value of relational missions as it relates to your discipleship.

- What mission work are you currently involved in through the church? What possible shifts might you like to make to make relationships a priority in your mission work?

- What mission work are you currently involved in through other community groups? Might there be opportunities for church partnership with your group?

Questions for the Pastor and Staff

- Is there a current mission team/committee? If so, describe the type of mission's work they promote?

- Describe the first step in moving your church from a church who does good things *for* people to becoming a church who relationally engages in mission work *with* others.

- What retooling might the staff and/or pastor need in making the shift to mission with IMPACT?

Chapter Six

Worship That Makes
An IMPACT

Everyone around was in awe – all those wonders and signs done through the apostles! And all the believers lived in a wonderful harmony, holding everything in common. They sold whatever they owned and pooled their resources so that each person's need was met.

They followed a daily discipline of worship in the Temple followed by meals at home, every meal a celebration, exuberant and joyful, as they praised God. People in general liked what they saw. Every day their number grew as God added those who were saved.

Acts 2:43-47 (The Message)

We sometimes struggle with the "why" of worship. How many times have we heard something to the effect of "worship just does not fill me up for the week." Or perhaps you may have heard something like "worship does not meet my needs."

What is the true purpose of worship? Many churches are filled with people who choose to watch worship. Others desire a worship experience that is experiential and participatory. In the book *Building Worship Bridges* by Townley, Kotan & Farr, worship is described as a bridge connecting the church to and from the community. [27] Worship sends believers out to connect with the community and bring believers and guests back to the gathered community.

In our scripture that opened this chapter, the earliest disciples worshiped together by praying, breaking bread, and sharing life together. Worship is a *verb* not a *noun*. Authentic and compelling worship is participatory, not a spectator sport. Worship is about praising God together as a community of believers. Worship should be compelling, should make an impact on our souls, and be a means of grace whereby God sends the worshipper out for ministry.

Laity IMPACT in Worship

Worship with IMPACT involves an experience of all the senses. Different people experience Christ in worship in a variety of ways. Worship with IMPACT provides opportunities for a variety of people to experience Christ. Some experience Christ in prayer, others with music, or maybe the message, prayer, scripture, liturgy, video, printed mate-

---

27 Townley, Cathy, Kay Kotan, Robert Farr. *Building Worship Bridges: Accelerating Neighborhood Connections Through Worship*. Market Square Publishing, 2017.

rial, or a take-home devotional resources. It is impossible for one clergy person to continuously create an IMPACTFUL worship experience solo. Solo-planned worship becomes stale and predictable.

Regardless of how you describe worship, compelling and IMPACTFUL worship is best planned with a team - a team of both clergy and laity. *Liturgy* actually means the work of the people. Too often, worship has instead been left up to the "pros" (clergy and music minister). A solo pastor, especially in the first year of ministry in a setting, is often planning worship for a community that she does not completely know or understand. I (Blake) vividly recall my first Easter morning at a church. I had served that congregation for months, and (I thought) I had asked all the right questions. I was doing the final set-up when one of the choir members arrived early to prepare. She asked me, "Where is the living cross." Huh? "The living cross. Every Easter we all bring flowers from our yards and gardens to place them in this wooden cross that has chicken wire on it." So to the storage room we went, until, sure enough, we found a large wooden box in the shape of the cross with chicken wire on the front of it. We managed to get it in place just before the crowd walked into the sanctuary.

We never published anything about bringing flowers in any of the previous weeks' bulletins or newsletter my first year, but almost everyone brought their flowers to place in the cross during the prelude. The laity knew their traditions; it was their clergy (me) that was clueless. I could have preached the best sermon and we could have sung all the favorite Easter Hymns, but I knew that the church would have a roasted preacher for the Sunday dinner if I had neglected their beloved Easter tradition. By "taking care of business" in planning all the congregation's worship, I was

Stand you / reading of the / Gospel

leaving out the voices of the laity, and setting myself up for failure. Lesson learned: worship leadership is meant to be shared between clergy and laity.

Laity provide a plethora of spiritual gifts. Too often those gifts are not utilized for the weekly worship experience. We often use the musical talents (vocal and instrumental) of our laity, but we often overlook other giftedness. Laity often bring other unique talents such as creativity, aesthetics and decor, resourcing video and graphics, thematic ideas, planning, organization, and bringing topics for sermon consideration based on community needs.

One of the best practices for using laity to plan worship is to create a worship design team. The team comes together periodically to dream, plan, strategize, create and resource worship with IMPACT. This team provides a unique gathering of people who can bring together worship from a variety of potential lenses for worship gifts and experiences in order to provide worship with IMPACT. Imagine throwing out a sermon series idea and allowing this team to take it from a word or phrase into a full-on worship experience over a four to six week period. I (Blake) would usually take retreat time every August to plan the following year's sermon series. I would bring my rough draft schedule back for the worship design team to work the content, and then we would lock it in, allowing staff and lay leaders in music ministries, decor, and young people's ministries to creatively shape the larger IMPACT of the worship experience. Our choirmaster even composed new hymn stanzas to fit better into the overall theme of worship. There is so much potential, power, creativity and opportunity in working together in a collaborative group.

Not only is this a gift for the pastor, it is also a gift for those being able to utilize their gifts in meaningful ways and a gift to the congregation for creating worship with IMPACT! Check out Kay's *Gear Up* and *Building Worship Bridges* by Townley, Kotan & Farr for more help on worship design.

Not only are there opportunities for laity to create worship, there are other opportunities to IMPACT worship leadership, too. Gone are the days where the congregation desires to have the pastor lead the entire worship service as a master of ceremonies. Rather, people engage at a deeper level when multiple folks including laity lead worship. Opportunities for laity to lead worship include such things as responsive readings, serving as worship leader or worship host, reading a poem or story, drama, dance, vocals, running sound and multimedia as well as instrumentalists and more.

A note of caution: Please equip the laity for their role in worship. Nothing is worse than asking a lay person to step up and then put him/her in a position of being embarrassed by not equipping him/her for the role. Furthermore, the people in the pews (and in particular new people) need to be able to identify with the leaders serving in the chancel or on the stage. In other words, put the people upfront in worship who look and live like the people you are trying to reach in the neighborhood. It is all about providing excellence in worship and matching worship leadership to those who you are trying to reach.

Horizontal and Vertical Worship

Planning worship is layered. Worship is one continuous experience with multiple encounters tied together. Worship with IMPACT is seamless with smooth transitions and elements that fit together as different puzzle pieces to create a crystal clear picture of the Gospel take-away for the day. IMPACTFUL worship causes us to think and act. It prompts transformation.

Worship is multi-dimensional. It takes laity to create these layers and dimensions. It is almost impossible for pastors alone to provide all the layers and dimensions needed to create and sustain dynamic, relevant, and contextual worship week after week.

Worship is horizontal. Worship is gathering people *together* to worship God. Worship is equipping laity for the works of the ministry. Worship is about sending people out. The sending is to transform the world. The sending is to share Jesus Christ with others so that they might come to know him. The sending out result in the gathering of those transformed back to the community of believers.

Worship is vertical. Worship is the act of praising God. Worship is also about being transformed by God's grace.

Worship with IMPACT is multi-layered, multi-dimensional, vertical and horizontal. IMPACTFUL worship requires laity's gifts and commitment. What elements might need to be considered to take your worship experience up a notch to have a more IMPACTFUL worship experience?

From Attractional to Missional

Too often churches have continued to rely on the attractional model for growth. In particular, the attractional model is most likely all about the Sunday morning experience. If the worship experience is great, the model assumes that people would come. If we have the best ministries, people will flock to the church. While the attractional model is not necessarily dead, the attractional model is much less effective than it once was. When we lived in a church-centric world, the attractional model was much more effective. In today's world, the attractional model usually only works for larger churches who have done the hard missional work of getting to know their neighborhood and connect in relevant ways to reach new people. Larger churches who still have some success with the attractional model usually also still have lots and lots of people engaged in ministry and there is a real "buzz" in the community because of the church's missional IMPACT.

When the attractional model worked, we assumed that Sunday morning worship was the front door that all members and potential members entered. From this experience in congregational worship, guests would then be expected to join a Sunday School class and help out in ministries. Worship was the hub around which all other ministries connected. Again, a few churches in parts of the country are still able to operate this attractional style, but people today connect in some sort of relational way with a small group, mission, activity, *or* worship. The person's relationships are now at the center or hub, and worship is one of the ways the relationship is expressed. This has made worship planning more complicated. When you add the changes in worship attendance frequency, the situation becomes even more complicated. For example, it is exceedingly difficult to design thematic worship components around a multi-week sermon series when active members attend only one or two Sundays a month. Individuals may continue to feel very connected to their small group or mission team, but just happen to be absent at half of the worship experiences. By including more laity in the planning and leadership of worship, you are not only creating a more compelling worship experience, you are creating more relational ties (e.g., our small group leader is today's liturgist!) that encourage a larger slice of the congregation to show up and engage with the worship experience.

While most churches would love to live into the attractional model, most simply are just not there yet, and frankly, the days of this model's fruitfulness are finite. The attractional model of church growth has an expectation of "y'all come." For most churches in most parts of the country, this simply does not work. Rather than rely on this most-often ineffective attractional model to reach new people, most churches need to consider moving to a missional model to reach new people. A missional church focuses all of their resources on how everything in the church aligns with its mission of making disciples of Jesus Christ for the transformation of the world. No longer would a missional church believe new people will come to conform to *who we are* and *what we desire* inside the church. Instead, a missional church does whatever is necessary to provide a place for people to experience Christ in a relevant, contextual way. Gone are the days of "my way or the highway" when it comes to worship. Rather, a missional church is eager and ready to create a meaningful worship experience for the unchurched. In addition, a missional church has no expectation for people to "show up" (but great if they do). A missional church is a sent out church to build relationships in the neighborhood and bring them back to the gathered community of believers. Being a missional church is a church full of laity who IMPACT the community by building relationships through ministry and inviting neighbors back to the gathered community to experience Christ.

New Worship Experiences

Many churches desire a new worship experience. The reasons are varied but might include a desire for different music styles, orders of worship, or venues. Too many times the desires spring up from a disconnect internally rather than our hearts breaking for our neighbors who do not yet know Jesus Christ. To make matters worst, we often fool ourselves into thinking that a new worship experience will suddenly bring in new people. This is simply not the case. Every new worship experience needs to be treated as a new church start and planted where relationships with new people in the community are built. There should be a gathering of new people intentionally in some way before there is any work in creating a new worship experience to help these new people experience Christ. I (Blake) tried starting a new worship service at a church that had reached its seating capacity in its main service without doing this important gathering work first, relying on the attractional model. It ended up reducing the fruitfulness of the worshiping congregations and we had to shut it down within months. Designing a turnkey "new worship service" without engaging the larger community first is the attractional model's way of meeting up with an inwardly focused church, dooming the entire enterprise for a disappointing outcome.

If a new worship experience is a part of your church's vision, the highest potential for a favorable outcome of reaching new people is if the vision becomes lay-driven and developed by a team. For far too long, the church planting process has been focused on the leadership of the clergy and consultants (either private or judicatory staff) and have

103

excluded the voice and wisdom of the mission congregation's existing laity. Some of the best new worship expressions are lay-led. How will your church begin to empower and equip laity to create new expressions of worship and faith? We also plead to church planters, judicatory staff, and new start consultants: please include lay leadership in your coaching and decision making!

There are multiple means of creating new expressions of worship that are lay-led. These include a new worship experience in an existing church, dinner church, cowboy church, church in a bar, church in a gym, yoga church, house churches, etc. The possibilities are endless. They are only limited by the passions of the laity when they are unleashed and empowered to create new expressions of worship and faith. We must simply begin to think about creating new places for new people using laity rather than always defaulting back to new worship expressions or new churches as exclusively a "clergy job."

order of worship

Planning Your IMPACT

Questions for the Lay Leadership/Board Member

- Describe the worship planning process in your church. What is the clergy/staff/laity balance in your congregation's worship design planning process? What changes, if any, might you consider after reading this chapter?

- In their book *Overflow: Increase Worship Attendance & Bear More Fruit,* Lovett Weems and Tom Berlin ask why churches of all sizes manage to figure out the giving records of members and use these records as an indicator of stewardship, but few congregations seem to actually track worship attendance with any precision or intentionality.[28] How might your board or leadership team utilize your congregation's worship attendance statistics (including comparing current numbers with statistics from over the past 3-5 years) to influence strategic decisions, evaluate your connections and discipleship processes, and inform your allocation of resources?

- How might your church begin to empower laity for new expressions of worship/faith?

Questions for the Disciple

- Explain your experience of worship in church. How multi-dimensional is your experience?

- What spiritual gifts might you have to offer to create a worship experience with IMPACT?

---

28 Berlin, Tom, and Lovett H. Weems. *Overflow: Increase Worship Attendance And Bear More Fruit.* Nashville: Abingdon Press, 2013, p. 14

Questions for the pastor and staff

- With brutal honesty, evaluate your current worship experience (this is not about blaming, but about seeking fruitfulness). How are laity being utilized in their areas of giftedness? What shifts need to be made to create worship with IMPACT?

- Is there a worship design team in your church? If so, how is it working? What needs to improve? Who is missing from the conversation? If you don't have a team, discuss the reasons, and imagine the opportunities if one were created.

- Describe how laity are consistently invited into the worship experience (current and future worship experiences). How could there be a more intentional plan and process to empower laity around worship?

Chapter Seven

IMPACT-Focused Lay Leadership

Jethro, Moses' father-in-law, brought a Whole-Burnt-Offering and
sacrifices to God. And Aaron, along with all the elders of Israel,
came and ate the meal with Moses' father-in-law in the presence
of God. The next day Moses took his place to judge the people.
People were standing before him all day long, from morning to
night. When Moses' father-in-law saw all that he was doing for
the people, he said, "What's going on here? Why are you doing all
this, and all by yourself, letting everybody line up before you from
morning to night?"

Moses said to his father-in-law, "Because the people come to me
with questions about God. When something comes up, they come
to me. I judge between a man and his neighbor and teach them
God's laws and instructions."

Moses' father-in-law said, "This is no way to go about it. You'll
burn out, and the people right along with you. This is way too
much for you – you can't do this alone. Now listen to me. Let me
tell you how to do this so that God will be in this with you. Be
there for the people before God, but let the matters of concern be
presented to God. Your job is to teach them the rules and instructions, to show them how to live, what to do. And then you need to
keep a sharp eye out for competent men – men who fear God, men
of integrity, men who are incorruptible – and appoint them as
leaders over groups organized by the thousand, by the hundred,
by fifty, and by ten. They'll be responsible for the everyday work
of judging among the people. They'll bring the hard cases to you,
but in the routine cases they'll be the judges. They will share your
load and that will make it easier for you. If you handle the work
this way, you'll have the strength to carry out whatever God com-
mands you, and the people in their settings will flourish also."

Exodus 18:12-23 (The Message)

107

Lay Leadership has been marginalized in today's church. In Chapter One, we shared that the church has become pastor-dependant. Due to this, lay leadership development has ceased to exist in most churches. Instead members' names fill slots required by denominational polity. Some positions need filling simply because we have always had somebody in the job, so now it is expected if "we really care about the ministry." Most often, expectations and responsibilities are not clear. But the paperwork is complete, so we suppose that is something! For some roles, there is a term of service; for others, it might be a lifetime sentence. When a list of responsibilities is included by the nominating committee, it is often a generic to-do list and rarely shares the potential or expected impact of the team's or committee's work. With such vagueness surrounding lay leadership roles, there is a reluctance to serve. When folks do agree to fill the slot and serve, they often do so halfheartedly and/ or because of the relationship they have with the person who asked him/her to serve. In our service in churches and denominational work around the nation, we have seen huge investments in clergy leadership, but relatively little is invested in laity, especially congregational *teams* of laity that can make an IMPACT.

Most of our United Methodist congregations are family-sized churches with 50 worship attenders or less showing up each week. In recent years, many churches have found themselves with their matriarch or patriarch -- the de facto leader of the last 40 or 50 years - becoming homebound or joining the heavenly rolls. Because these senior leaders have served in these key leadership roles for decades, little work was done to mentor or intentionally develop new leaders for the important work of connecting the church to the mission field. This has

left a monumental void in strategic leadership. In the midst
of this leadership void, the remainder of the church's leaders
are coming to terms with a new problem: there is no denominational policy for "inheriting" a church!

In some churches, leadership was a place of honor rather
than a position matched to spiritual gifts and calling. Nominating committees first thought about the people of influence
in the church and then made sure that all these influential
members were slotted to fill some blank space on the leadership chart. Rotating off one committee (if the church even
bothered to have annual classes) simply meant that you
would now begin on a new committee. Traditional roles in
leadership in decades past had great influence for the worship
order and had great reverence for the church building/facil-
ity. The budget would reflect these concerns with the lion's
share of resources being spent on traditional worship and the
maintenance needs of the congregation's facility. Much importance was given to the *role* of being a leader as a key influ-
encer rather than the *responsibility* of the collective church
leadership to guide the congregation in making an IMPACT
for Christ. Leadership became more of a position of honor and
prestige. Community and business leaders had an *expectation*
of also being a church leaders – even if only in name.

There is a better way to imagine
lay leadership that makes an IMPACT....

In contrast to the "norm" of leadership of decades past,
today's leader is interested in a new form of leadership. An
effective modern leader is looking to lead with simplicity
and authenticity. This leader desires barrier-free leading,
a permission-giving environment to explore and experi-

ment within safe, identified healthy boundaries. Excellent communication with expectations and responsibilities are expected and valued. Most importantly, today's modern leader wants to lead where IMPACT can be made. Long gone are the days of the modern leader desiring to serve in a role only in name.

Let me (Blake) share a personal story that may be helpful. A few years ago, our family took over hosting duties for Thanksgiving dinner. It was not a planned inheritance, arranged over a series of seasons. Instead, my mother had been quite ill that fall and simply wasn't up the enormous task of cooking and preparing for everyone. A change in hosting leadership meant many changes in the expected menu. A beef roast replaced the turkey. My wife's north Arkansas mashed potatoes replaced the traditional south Arkansas rice. Our vegetarian daughter created several dishes that did not include meat or meat products (a difficult task in the south were every veggie seems to include at least one meat ingredient). Finally, our setting was more casual due to space differences in our homes. The meal was well received, and the "leadership transition" seemed to go over well. Of course, when my mother recovered in a few months, she also wanted us to come over for a *turkey dinner* at her house as soon as possible. Which of course, we did gladly! The next year, we sent some feelers out -- would it be helpful if we hosted Thanksgiving again that year? "Yes" was the answer. And, some new traditions were born. Leadership transitions are always complicated in families or in the extended families that make up a congregational community. There will usually be some hesitant steps forward and perhaps even a few steps back. But new leadership must always be nurtured for the next generation.

Governance

How a church is structured to make decisions really should matter to the IMPACTFUL leader. The structure needs to be clear, simple, and enable actual decisions. Multi-layered, time-consuming decision-making will be stumbling blocks for new leaders to become involved. The inherited system of multiple committees is designed for an era of maintenance, not mission. In many ways, our traditional committee process of decision-making is perfectly designed for *nothing* to happen, with one or two powerful voices able to completely shut down creative ideas. Even worse is the bicameral legacy model of an administrative board and council on ministries, a model used by many congregations which places two separate bodies in competition with one another for power and authority of the church's mission. In this system, *everyone* is responsible for the church's mission and vision in a way that actually *no one* is held responsible. Without a clear, accountable leadership team, the church will stay stuck in a maintenance mode, with new ideas stuck in an endless loop.

If the process of moving from ministry *idea* to ministry *implementation* is too cumbersome, today's leaders will opt out. Gone are the days where a church can take four to six months running decisions through multiple committees to make critical decisions. Our world works at a much quicker pace today, and we are living in a post-Christendom culture that simply won't wait for the church to catch up. Leaders are looking to work within a governance process where real and greater IMPACT can be experienced routinely.

Modern leaders desire the opportunity to mobilize fellow laity for missional IMPACT. That is IMPACT that ties directly

111

to the mission and vision of the church. Leaders want to connect the dots of their ministry tied directly to the big picture of the church's purpose. Today's leaders, especially millennials, desire the opportunity to make a real difference in the community, not fill a slot on a denominational form. Modern leaders will not invest their gifts, time and energy in activities that do not make a real difference. They desire effective and efficient God-sized IMPACT!

Churches desiring to recruit and equip modern leaders will likely need to shift into the simplified, accountable leadership structure. This is often called a single-board model of governance (although using that terminology can be misleading), in which all the ongoing administrative and strategic functions of leadership are delegated to a single executive team. For United Methodists (our branch of the Christian family tree) this structure is enabled by the UMC *Book of Discipline* ¶ 247.2 (2016). Leaders seeking IMPACT value the efficiency and effectiveness of the four administrative teams -- finance, personnel (Staff/Pastor Parish Relations), property (Trustees), and administrative board -- combining into a single governance team. This simplification of your structure allows a streamlined and clear line of accountability:

- The governance responsibilities of fiduciary, generative, and strategic work take priority in the lay leadership team's work.
- The management of the day-to-day church should be the responsibility of the pastor and staff (paid and unpaid).
- The laity of the church are equipped for ministry.

When the council/board is involved in day-to-day management decisions, no one is left to focus on governing. In other words, everyone is taking care of the day-to-day business (and getting into each other's way, causing unnecessary conflict), but no one is doing the big-picture work of making sure the church is living out its purpose of building disciples who disciple others.

When leadership moves to the simplified, accountable leadership structure, the church begins to align all its resources to the congregation's mission and unique vision. Those resources include such things as time, energy, people, facility, budget, and calendar. With a clearly stated purpose and trajectory, leadership is freed from the outdated burden of making decisions based on the singular priority of maintaining positive personal relationships with each other. Instead decisions are made for missional alignment. The strategic work of aligning our church, its members, and its resources toward its purpose of making disciples becomes the sole focus of the governing board. Policies and guidelines are created to allow permission-giving to ministries and new ideas to ensure both congregational alignment and missional IMPACT.

The policies and guiding principles become the traffic guard rails for the church ministries, keeping the church on the road toward fulfilling its mission. Individual decisions by the board/council on every ministry are no longer required. Monthly presentation and reports certainly are not required. Instead, permission-giving guidelines are provided and decisions are made easily with flexibility without the board/council micromanaging every decision. Whenever the governance team does make a decision, it also needs to ask itself, "Should this be a new standing guideline so that no one has to wait on us to make a decision next time?"

Assessment, evaluation, and reflection are critically

important to a healthy governance model when practicing accountable leadership. We must become proficient with assessment at every level. The board is accountable to Christ for the church living its mission of making disciples. The pastor is accountable to the board for the church's annual goals and living into its vision of God's preferred future for how it uniquely makes disciples. The staff (paid and unpaid ministry leaders) are accountable to the pastor for the day-to-day ministry, with the pastor ensuring that the ministries are aligned with the church's annual goals. Constant and consistent evaluation at all levels is critical to enable the church to assess its fruitfulness and remain in alignment of its purpose/mission. Finally, the board needs to take time to reflect on ministries and their effectiveness. Accountability is not about blaming, but its certainly about *learning*. An organization that never reflects on their work never learns or adapts. A word of warning: Evaluation and accountability are key, but please know that this is an incredibly difficult shift to live into because it will take persistence and patience, but it will be so worth the investment!

A common metaphor for describing governance and management structures is that of the playground. Before moving to my role in our conference (judicatory) office, my (Blake's) last church built a new playground in cooperation with our after-school and summer camp ministry, so I became well acquainted with the subject of playgrounds. For instance, I found out that developing the site, creating the foundation, and fencing in the playground costs much more money and takes much more time than the construction of the actual playground equipment. Our playground was in a complicated location. We had a small ditch nearby, woods surrounding the lot, an elementary school on one side, and a cliff on the other side. To use the language of governance and management, we knew the mission and the vision of a playground. We want the children to use it because physical exercise and cooperative play outdoors is a nurturing experience. And the after-school ministry has a responsibility to safely supervise and nurture the children under its care. In this metaphor, a church's policies, guiding principles, and governance architecture are the foundation and fencing of the playground: they mark the difference of what is allowed and what is out of bounds. Inside, the fun happens -- the playground is fulfilling its vision. Outside the fence can be a bit dangerous and it is unsupervised. Along with the governance and policy "fencing," individual playground equipment may have rules. One rule may focus on the use of the slides. Other rules may involve waiting one's turn. These rules or guidelines are less formal than the fencing around the playground, and are devised by the childcare staff to manage the children's experience (for example, to make sure everyone shares, takes turns, and doesn't go headfirst down the slide). Our churches have guidelines or standard practices as well, and these are usually created by ministry team leaders or staff to manage the daily use of the church's resources and meet the needs of the day. While not as formal as the policy fences, these guidelines are just as amenable to the congregation's policies and the governing board, and these guidelines must be written with the church's missional IMPACT as the focus.

While we heartily recommend a simplified, and an accountable leadership structure, please know that fewer people making decisions is not the goal, nor is a new governance architecture a silver bullet. The goal is, and should always be, making an IMPACT for Christ. Changing the number of people around the leadership table without also changing the leadership *culture* will only result in an isolated and ineffective board. Shifting to a new governance model is both a technical and an adaptive change. We can imagine (and get quite excited about) moving to fewer number of people sitting around the board table and having fewer meetings. Amen! Fewer people and less meetings is the easy part. This is the technical change. However, for real IMPACT to occur, we must also make the necessary *adaptive* changes. Adaptive changes are those changes we cannot truly imagine how they might work without cooperation and exploration. Adaptive work causes us to learn new behaviors and act in different ways. The adaptive shifts for simplified, accountable leadership requires us to adopt a new kind of agenda, have different conversations around the table, and focus on different aspects of the church than we have before. Shifting from management to governance conversations will be difficult. Yet, this is a critical shift in moving to leadership with IMPACT!

If you are moving to the simplified, accountable leadership structure or have adopted this model but are struggling to implement it, check out Kay's book, *Mission Possible: Structuring Your Church for Missional Effectiveness*. This book offers help with the following:

- The "why" of moving to this new governance model.
- How to move to the new model.
- The role of the new board.
- A suggested new agenda to help steer the conversation adaptively.
- Examples of guiding principles.
- Example of a Leadership Covenant.

- A typical rhythm of leadership throughout the annual calendar for church leadership.

Whatever structure you adopt for IMPACT, make sure it is designed for a church your size and is built for your future, not your past. I (Blake) once visited with a church of 70 that had continued to operate with all the committees and ministry teams they had when they worshipers were 250. Understandably, they were exhausted trying to keep up the ministry tempo, the meeting schedule, and the internal expectations of their former selves. During a season when they were receiving a new pastoral appointment, they took the opportunity to rethink their structure, and released their members from meetings so that they could engage in more IMPACTFUL ministry.

Meetings are important, but they should not be confused with *ministry* (this will come as a great shock to all our fellow Methodists). So, imagine making the most of your leadership time together. Dump the endless reports (reports should all be emailed before the meeting as part of consent calendar) and use your limited time in meetings for strategic work. Your leadership team needs to have the space and time to look beyond the church's walls, to examine the needs of the community, and to spend time in deep prayer and discernment. Look at big picture. What should be the congregation's next steps that would make a real Kingdom IMPACT? It is out of this discernment process and clear strategy that new ministries are approved and ineffective ministries are "laid to rest" (again, well done, good and faithful ministry). The leadership is then enabled to spend time evaluating ministries and reflecting upon your ministries, learning from them, and holding other leaders accountable to your church's larger vision and strategic plan.

Congregational Health

Being the church is oftentimes hard work. This is especially true in today's unchurched world. We often fool ourselves that being a "healthy church" equates to a church having no conflict. Quite the contrary is true. A church with no disagreements is a church that is making no decisions. Healthy organizations have conflict. Having no conflict most often equates to little or no missional IMPACT. It is *how* a church manages conflict that is most important. When a church is playing too safe, avoiding conflict, then it loses IMPACT and its very way. Healthy churches have healthy conflict that pushes the envelope and keeps the church relevant and compelling in their mission field.

Congregations need functioning and nurtured "immune systems" to stay healthy. A congregation cannot depend upon the pastor to serve as the congregation's immune system. While the pastor may have some role to play in transforming conflict in her capacity as a spiritual leader, it is really the congregation's lay leadership that provides the church with the antibodies to protect the congregation's mission. The body needs to work together to promote and protect a healthy immune system. For a congregation, that means that the lay leadership need to provide relational boundaries, such as rejecting the use of secret meetings, gossip, bullying, blaming, shaming, and triangulation. An example of triangulation is a member coming to you to "fix" the pastor and rebuffing any suggestion to go to the pastor directly. Another circumstance in which lay leadership must be proactive in creating and nurturing health is when influential members seek to bypass the congregation's policies, processes, or guidelines. When a governing board has set policy, we must back up our pastor when she seeks to enforce our policy. To do otherwise not only undermines the pastor, but also destroys the trust of the entire congregation. Meanwhile the emotional anxiety of the congregation starts to rise. In order to clarify expectations, some boards and staffs even write behavioral and/or leadership covenants[29] to support one another and hold each other accountable in Christ-centered ways, often using Matthew 18 as their guide. In our work with congregations across the country, we have seen the disastrous consequences of church leadership failing to hold fellow lay members accountable for unhealthy behaviors. We have also seen this pain played out generationally, with bad behaviors distracting the church from God's mission again and again, and often placing the blame on decades worth of pastors. Friends, if this sounds familiar to your experience of your congregation, it is up to you as a lay leader to start changing the church's culture. Especially in situations where the pastor is new to a community, you have to be the antibodies that promote health, transparency, and accountability while being crystal clear about the congregation's plans to make an IMPACT in the name of Christ.

Immune systems can both be healthy and unhealthy. Healthy immune systems protect the body from viruses, bacteria, and diseases. Unhealthy immune systems can no longer protect the body from outside intrusions and sickness. For a church, destructive behaviors can enter into the life of the church. These destructive behaviors take the focus off healthiness, attacking and zapping the health of the organization. When the church's immune system itself is attacked, the church loses its focus on its missional IMPACT – its align-

---

29 See Gil Rendle's *Behavioral Covenants In Congregations: A Handbook For Honoring Differences*. Bethesda, Md: Alban Institute, 1999, for some examples and a process for clarifying expectations.

ment with the big picture of mission and vision. There are different kinds of unhealthy immune systems: An unhealthy immune system could be focusing on tradition and history and forgetting the congregation's mission. Another type of unhealthy congregational immune system may focus entirely on the happiness of a particular influential members.

One note about immune systems: they can be overactive. Normal stimulus (i.e cats or ragweed) should not cause a coughing, sneezing fit. Similarly, a church can easily overreact and see normal healthy conflict as dangerous and react in unhelpful ways. Also, some churches are in a situation where extreme action must be taken for the sake of Jesus Christ's mission. These big changes could cause quite a bit of blaming and other "immune system responses" My (Blake's) father had a heart transplant and was on anti-rejection drugs for some time. Without these important medicines, his immune system would attack his new heart. We have both seen churches' overactive immune systems reject pastors, new ideas, and new members outright, all to the detriment of the congregation's potential IMPACT for Christ.[30]

So, lay leadership needs to check out its immune systems. How does your church handle conflict? Does it seek to amplify, suppress, or *transform* conflict? Does conflict keep the church from its missional IMPACT or does the church manage conflict in a healthy manner? Does your church embody a healthy immune system? Does the health of your congregation create an environment for IMPACT?

---

30 The "congregational immune system" is part of the church's deeper culture. For a secular perspective on the power of culture, read Nilofer Merchant's article "Culture Trumps Strategy, Every Time," in the *Harvard Business Review*, March 22, 2011. See https://hbr.org/2011/03/culture-trumps-strategy-every. This concept has been shared in a popular quote attributed to management expert Peter Drucker: "Culture eats strategy for breakfast."

Pastoral Collaboration

The relationship of the pastor and the laity leaders is critical. We need to be partners in ministry. Understanding our distinctive roles in leadership is a must. In the accountable leadership model of governance, the board is accountable to Christ for the mission of the church. The pastor is accountable to the board for the vision and annual goals. The ministry leaders and ministry teams will be managed and coordinated by the pastor and staff, within the "fencing" and foundation of the congregation's vision, mission, policies, and overall goals. This is the most effective and efficient model for IMPACT!

The pastor's role is not one of church ownership nor is that the role of the lay leadership. Christ is the owner of the church; we should be owning the mission that Christ gave us. The board's role is governance and partnering with the pastor in the strategic work of visioning. The pastor's role is that of a leader and an equipper. It is vitally important for the roles to be clearly understood and implemented. When these roles are not understood or are flipped, the overall health of the church is at stake. The church will likely lose its way and its IMPACT!

I (Kay) often use the metaphor of the church being a charter bus on a trip. Imagine having prepared and equipped the passengers (lay leaders) for their trip. The right passengers (equipped and called laity leaders) are on the bus and in the right seats (serving in their spiritual giftedness). The driver comes aboard and programs the bus' GPS to the desired destination (mission and current vision). With any trip, there will likely be traffic congestion, construction, potholes, and maybe even detours (changes in community, new ministries, ministries that need to be retired, changing financial factors). Yet, the destination (mission) does not change. From time to time, the bus will come to a rest stop so the passengers can stretch their legs and get some fresh air. When the passengers climb back onto the bus, they realize the driver has changed (See Chapter Eight for more about leadership during a new pastoral appointment). The mission and vision did not change. We simply have a change of drivers. While we will miss our previous driver, we must continue on our mission to God's preferred future. IMPACT!

Mentoring for IMPACT

Without a clearly defined and intentional leadership development process, we as the church will struggle to have IMPACT! Leadership by happenstance is not intentional nor effective. Leadership development by begging someone to take an "office" is a process of desperation rather than an intentional leadership development process. We can and must do better to have IMPACT!

The most effective leadership development process is identifying people with potential leadership gifts prior to the need of leadership. The process helps one identify their gifts and then align their gifts with the ministry. Leaders are then equipped for the ministry they are serving. Equipping through mentoring is the most effective and efficient process. The mentoring process steps are:

1. I do. You watch. We talk.
2. I do. You help. We talk.
3. You do. I help. We talk.
4. You do. I watch. We talk.
5. You do. I move to mentor another.

Identifying, equipping and mentoring is the responsibility of all lay leaders. This is not the sole role of the pastor. We must build a culture of leadership development to have a healthy pipeline of equipped and called multi-generational leaders.

All clergy start as laypeople -- a fact often forgotten by pulpit search teams and Pastor/Parish Relations Committees. All churches desire competent, called, courageous and compelling clergy to serve. How many clergy has your church raised up (and how has your congregation supported them during their education)? How are we nurturing a culture of call? Some churches are using their confirmation programs and even third-grade bible distributions to explicitly share about the needs and hopes for a new generation of clergy. How are we especially nurturing our youth in exploring potential calls? We have seen several IMPACT-focused churches intentionally provide opportunities for youth to break out beyond the youth program silo to explore ministry through internships, leadership on ministry teams, and impactful engagement in the church and community not because they are youth, but because they are *disciples of Jesus Christ* who happen to be youth. Every new clergy person has to start with ministering their first church. How open is your church in mentoring and supporting a new clergy? What is the role of any associate pastors you might have? Are they being mentored and supported in their call to lead a local congregation?

A culture of calling and vocational discernment does not simply "happen". It must be included as part of the congregation's overall vision. Staff time and ministry team resources must be tasked to include it in your congregation's overall intentional discipleship process (Remember Chapter 3!). The language of invitation must be consistent, and the description of calling must be broad enough to include all kinds of ministry: lay, staff, licensed, and ordained. We are all ministers by our baptisms, and we must also create a culture for all to discern their spiritual gifts and calling.

Planning Your IMPACT

Questions for the Lay Leadership/Board Member

- How is the church leadership effectively aligned with its mission and vision for IMPACT?

- How does your church leadership get information? Is all information processed through the "laity grapevine" or through the biases, assumptions, and fears of the clergy leader? Imagine distributing an annual anonymous survey to all the laity of the church, along with a guest experience survey sent immediately to everyone who worships with your congregation for the first time. How might this kind of data lead your team to deeper and more productive conversations? What might be the IMPACT of this sort of feedback on your leadership priorities and assumptions?

- How well does the church handle conflict? What improvements might need to be made?

- Describe the mentoring process for leadership development and clergy call. How will your church have future IMPACT by nurturing a call to ministry?

Questions for the Disciple

- Read the scripture passage from Exodus that began this chapter. How does Jethro's leadership advice to Moses relate to your church's leadership? How are decisions being made? How is the responsibility for leadership being shared among laity and your clergy leader?

- What are my spiritual gifts for leadership? How am I using those gifts in my church?

- Who in the congregation am I being called to encourage and mentor as a future leader?

- How am I mentoring the next generation of leaders for my current ministry role?

Questions for the Pastor and Staff

- Describe the mentoring process for equipping people for leadership. What improvements might be needed?

- How does the role of each staff member play into the mission and vision of the church?

Chapter Eight

New Pastor's Arrival:
Opportunity for IMPACT

The guild of prophets at Jericho came to Elisha and said, "Did you know that God is going to take your master away from you today?" "Yes," he said, "I know it. But keep it quiet." Meanwhile, fifty men from the guild of prophets gathered some distance away while the two of them stood at the Jordan. Elijah took his cloak, rolled it up, and hit the water with it. The river divided and the two men walked through on dry land. When they reached the other side, Elijah said to Elisha, "What can I do for you before I'm taken from you? Ask anything." Elisha said, "Your life repeated in my life. I want to be a holy man just like you." "That's a hard one!" said Elijah. "But if you're watching when I'm taken from you, you'll get what you've asked for. But only if you're watching." And so it happened. They were walking along and talking. Suddenly a chariot of fire and horses of fire came between them and Elijah went up in a whirlwind to heaven. Elisha saw it all and shouted, "My father, my father! You – the chariot and cavalry of Israel!" When he could no longer see anything, he grabbed his robe and ripped it into two pieces. Then he picked up Elijah's cloak that had fallen from him, returned to the shore of the Jordan, and stood there. He took Elijah's cloak – all that was left of Elijah! – and hit the river with it, saying, "Now where is the God of Elijah? Where is he?" When he struck the water, the river divided and Elisha walked through. The guild of prophets from Jericho saw the whole thing from where they were standing. They said, "The spirit of Elijah lives in Elisha!" They welcomed and honored him.

2 Kings 2:5, 7-15 (The Message)

126

So, your pastor is leaving and a new pastor is arriving. What will be the transition plan for your congregation? Should you wait for the new pastor to get settled to move ahead on some large goals? How will you truly and intentionally welcome and connect your new pastor into the church and community? How might you leverage this mantle-passing moment to create momentum for evangelism efforts? These are strategic questions that will impact how proactive a role your congregation will take during a pastoral change.

The arrival of a new pastor is an amazing opportunity for the congregation to mobilize for IMPACT. Receiving a new pastor creates a window -- often a fleeting moment -- for your fellow members to look at your church with fresh eyes, assess its culture, and use the opportunity for some cultural shifts that could impact the congregation in your community. You can be intentional in how you describe your community, your mission field, and your church's culture to the new pastor. This in itself is huge -- and it requires a level of honesty and self-awareness. What makes the difference is the "why" behind your work on boarding a new pastoral leader. If the purpose is to simply help the new clergyperson to "get with the program" and "understand how things work around here," then the opportunity will be lost. On the other hand, if your purpose during this time of transition is to leverage the moment for serious Kingdom IMPACT, then all your critical conversations, providing of information, and intentional relationship building has the potential to produce amazing fruit!

LifeWay Research has found that the average pastoral tenure in a church today is between 4-6 years.[31] In our

---

31 Rainer, Thom. "Six Reasons Pastoral Tenure May Be Increasing." March 15, 2017. See http://thomrainer.com/2017/03/six-reasons-pastoral-tenure-may-be-increasing/.

denomination, the United Methodist Church, pastors are appointed or reappointed annually with retirements, seminary graduations, and multiple internal concurrent moves all happening every summer. Summer has become, for many congregations, a season of simultaneously saying goodbye and hello to pastoral leadership. Because compensation charts and "happy (or unhappy) churches" are no longer the norm for retention or moving of pastors, congregations are left trying to figure out words like "mission field compatibility" while their pastor is packing up her office and making a few last visits to homebound members before the moving van arrives. It is a time of high anxiety for the congregation. Even in call systems where congregational leaders retain a large degree of control over the pastoral search process, the unknown permeates the church's atmosphere and ministries. *Change* is expected, but that word *"change"* covers a lot of territory.

There has always been a disconnection between clergy and congregation when it comes to the idea of *"change."* Clergy keeps a stack of moving boxes in their attic until they retire because *change* is their expected norm. Every few years, clergy pack up everything they own, move to a new town (or even state), and show up at a new church and community mission field, with a Bible in one hand and an uncertain amount of emotional, spiritual, and literal baggage in the other. When clergy think about *change*, they don't have to work very hard to imagine changing every relationship, every personal business contact (from dentist to car mechanic), every ministry habit, and every other facet of their lives a few times every decade. Meanwhile, these change-adept clergies begin a new partnership with a congregation full of members that may be quite stable and relatively unchanging in their ways of "doing church." What laity may experience as a huge change, a shift in being, or a feeling of "starting from scratch" is simply not perceived as *"change"* by a clergyperson who rarely has time to unpack between moves. What flows from this disconnection about *change* is the potential for tragic misunderstandings during a pastoral transition.

I (Blake) have assisted with pastoral transition workshops for a number of years, but we always focused on the role of the clergy as they transition between churches. We often would spend a lot of time equipping pastors with tools to understand their new mission field, remind them that clergy needs to be open to learning new things because every church and community is unique, and offering methods that pastors could use to be more intentional about the first few months of their tenure.

At times, I felt like I was leading premarital counseling with only one half of the couple! A few judicatories are beginning to include a congregation's lay leadership in the transition process, either through inviting a group to a workshop or providing resources and equipping to designated transition teams that remain at work for the first 90 days or even the first full year of a new pastor's tenure. In their excellent book *The Changeover Zone: Successful Pastoral Transitions,*[32] Jim Ozier and Jim Griffith use the image of passing a relay race baton as a symbol of a pastoral transition. By taking ownership of Christ's vision for your congregation, you have an active role in the baton-passing between pastors. The pastoral transition season provides an opportu-

---

32 Ozier, Jim, and Jim Griffith. *The Changeover Zone: Successful Pastoral Transitions.* Nashville: Abingdon Press, 2016.

nity that your congregation cannot afford to miss. Remember, in the midst of all the personal feelings that we church members carry during a pastoral transition, including grief, worry, and sometimes relief, the congregation's mission field is still out there, beyond our walls and our stained glass, with countless souls needing the Gospel. During the pastoral transition season, with all the focus set squarely on getting to know the new pastor and helping the pastor know us, along with all the changes happening, the congregation can get self-focused and forget that making a God-sized IMPACT is the real goal. So, how can church leaders and disciples keep focused on and moving toward Christ-centered transformation while also saying hello and goodbye to pastoral leadership?

The Personnel Committee

In the United Methodist Church, the pastor-parish or staff/pastor parish relationship committee (S/PPRC) serves as the governing board overseeing personnel matters, including consultation with our judicatory officials -- the district superintendents and bishop. How this relationship exactly works varies wildly between conferences and particular Episcopal leaders. But in any form of this relationship with judicatory officials, especially in systems that send itinerant pastors, there are two keys: communication and self-awareness. We have seen congregations that assume that their district superintendent and bishop know their needs and mission field and never bother to share pertinent information. There are congregations that communicate a lot about their congregation's identity, but their perception of the church's identity (and sometimes even their attendance numbers!) is sorely out-of-date and shows a profound lack of self-awareness.

We often hear laity are frustrated that they must "start over" every time a new pastor is appointed. Yet we, as laity, must first own who we are and where God is leading us. Without that missional ownership and clear communication to the pastor about the mission, vision, core values and current congregational goals, pastors are left to create something on their own.

We find it interesting that many churches tell their district superintendent they desire a "young pastor with lots of energy" to reach bring in "children, youth, and their families" (a horribly ageist request, built on misguided assumptions). Yet, many times when a district superintendent and Bishop send such a pastor, the congregation is unwilling to adapt to the changes in the life of the church that would make any transformation possible. Make sure you are really willing and open to do a new thing for a new day to reach new, younger, and more diverse people. If we say we desire this with our lips, yet are unwilling or unable to take action to make the shifts, we only frustrate the pastor, the district superintendent, Bishop, and the congregation. Be careful what you ask for or you may just get it!

Interesting enough, the two key skills – communication and self-awareness – that make the difference in the search or placement process with judicatory officials also are the very same skills that will make the difference in how a new pastor begins her or his ministry. Lay passivity during the pastoral transition creates a situation where a pastor, no matter how gifted, is required to make a huge amount of assumptions and decisions that could go very badly very quickly. Some judicatories, building upon the excellent advice of Bob Kaylor's excellent advice for pastors in *Your Best Move*,[33] are requiring that a transition task force is created that works internationally before, during and after a clergy transition. A best practice is for the S/PPRC, board, or other designated transition team to meet *monthly* with the new pastor. The monthly meetings should focus on two areas: communication and self-awareness. Blake has a sample of monthly S/PPRC agenda items on his website, blakebradford.org.

Communication

Communication begins well before a new pastor is appointed or arrives. While the members of the personnel committee, S/PPRC, or transition team may all understand their denomination's polity and expectations regarding a pastoral transition, in our post-denominational culture, there are probably a lot of incorrect assumptions being made when it is announced that a pastor is moving or retiring. So, the transition process needs to be clearly outlined. Folks will understand that there are a lot of confidential issues involved in a transition process, but the process itself should be completely transparent, and the personnel committee should take the primary leadership role in educating the congregation about the process. During the selection or appointment process, the expectations and hopes outlined in your congregational profile could be shared with the larger congregation so that the committee can test its assumptions and plans with a larger slice of the congregation. By communicating the S/PPRC's profile before a new pastor's name is attached, you are preparing the congregation for the incoming pastor's ministry. All this preliminary communication

33 Kaylor, Robert. *Your Best Move: Effective Leadership Transition for the Local Church*. Franklin, Tennessee: Asbury Seedbed Publishing, 2013.

will hopefully lessen the anxiety of the congregation.

Communication must be multidirectional, including the pastors, the S/PPRC, the appointive cabinet, and the congregation. The word *relations* in the title of the Staff/Pastor Parish Relations Committee is meaningful because their primary work is *relational*, so the committee's communications should be as much about listening as talking, like in any healthy relationship. When we as laity are not intentional about communicating the needs, expectations, and culture of the congregation, we really are setting up a new pastor to fail. In the healthiest transitions, the S/PPRC or transition team serves as a two-way interpreter between the congregation and the new pastor: clarifying expectations and feedback, identifying the congregation's sacred cows and blessed traditions, and connecting the new pastor to the congregation and community with intentional introductions.

While the elected officers are charged with this responsibility, this interpretive role is not limited to the officers of the church! Every disciple in the pew has a responsibility to assist during a clergy leader transition. New pastors are constantly trying to figure out how to lead your congregation in making a Kingdom IMPACT, but they are unsure of the levers of power and authority. New pastors don't know the relationships, the community's needs, the congregation's landmines and past failures, or even what day the garbage is picked up at the parsonage. Instead of reflexively demanding adherence with the established tradition or protocol, ask the new pastor "why" questions to seek out deeper reasons for their actions. The action or change a new pastor brings could be simply a habit of the new pastor, a well-intentioned blunder, or part of an intentional mission-focused plan.

"Why" questions (from a curiosity perspective rather

than from judgment) move you both from the realm of assumptions or the blame-game and lead to real communication. Because they have a much different perspective, the newly arrived clergy simply do not understand that the changes that they bring can feel (to longtime members) like seismic shifts or even a disorienting culture of starting everything over. Along the way, the newly arrived clergyperson is trying mightily to become *your pastor*, not simply *the preacher*. By being open and honest with your communication and feedback, you are blessing your pastor and the entire congregation.

Know Thyself

The Greek philosopher Socrates encouraged his students to "know thyself." As coaches and consultants to congregations, we believe that the best experts of the "community mission field" are the leaders in the mission field. However, we have also seen very few church boards and leadership teams have a clear and consistent awareness of the congregation's current status and trajectory. We have also seen too many church boards willfully ignore statistics about worship attendance, outreach participation, discipleship groups, and professions of faith. While these statistics, or congregational vital signs, may feel like disconnected numbers that don't tell the story of the congregation's life (there is quite a bit of controversy in church leadership circles about how to measure, count, understand and interpret congregational statistics) these numbers are important. The numbers represent Missional IMPACT! The numbers represent souls. Tracking all the statistics weekly is one way of staying tied to the reality of our IMPACT and our trajectory, and holding ourselves accountable to the mission that Christ has for us. By tracking weekly, you get the data you really need to make it actionable: identifying *trends*. The story of early Methodism in Britain and America is filled with descriptions of accountability for our impact in the world. Souls mattered, and we measure what matters to us, so numbers were recorded and lay and clergy alike were held accountable. Why would we expect any less of ourselves today? We need to know what kind of IMPACT we are making for Christ so that we can be honest with denominational leaders, potential pastors and ourselves about the congregation's trajectory, so that we can set a clear baseline of expectations to hold the board and a new pastor accountable once the pastor arrives.

A change in clergy leadership is also a perfect time to begin a tradition of a congregational survey. Surveys often create a bit of anxiety on the part of the clergy. While, as the adage "information is your friend" may be true, what people do with the information is not always friendly. But the arrival of a new pastor creates a window for lay leadership to get some critical information and identify your next steps. Perhaps now is a great time to establish a new tradition for an annual survey (aka congregational inventory) that is more about the future than the past, which allows members to prioritize goals, and that offers the congregation an opportunity to share how the Spirit may be nudging them to impact lives, your community, and the world through Christ's church. Grab the moment to listen to one another and help foster a new and healthy culture of lay-clergy partnership. Receiving a new pastor does not have to feel like starting over, but a healthy lay leadership team can work with a new pastor to turn this moment of disruption into the season of transformation -- both inside and beyond the walls of the church.

Of course, all your work toward congregational self-awareness is not an end unto itself -- it's about making an IMPACT! Self-awareness is one element in allowing the greatest IMPACT to occur. Your congregation, no matter who the pastor, will never live up to the vision that God has for you without knowing your special place in the body of Christ, your congregation's unique calling to service in and with your community, and how ministry is conceived and implemented among your leadership.

Know Thy Community, Too!

A new pastor needs to know more than the locations of parishioners' homes and "the general lay of the land." New pastors need us to share our knowledge of the mission field and identify possible levers for IMPACT. Before we can describe our community or neighborhood to a new or potential pastor, we better make sure that our assessment of the community is up-to-date. We may think we know the demographics of the neighborhood, but we may also be remembering how the community used to be. This community disconnect is very common when the congregation primarily commutes into the church from another area. A district superintendent friend of ours recently visited a congregation as they were composing their congregational profile, in order to have the best pastoral match. He asked what the congregation was doing about ministering alongside the large Pacific Islander immigrant community that had settled nearby the last five years. The congregation was in disbelief -- they simply had not noticed the huge demographic shifts right under their noses. He had to bring a set of MissionInsite reports and maps so they could unpack the community's growing diversity. While we go along with our friendship circles, jobs, and everyday activities (including lots of church activities), the world outside is shifting.

The shifts in our communities are occurring everywhere: As we shared in Chapter Two, census data says that the U.S. population will become majority-minority in 2044. Meanwhile, all the Baby Boomers will retire by 2029[34] and the middle class has shrunk as a percentage of the U.S. population over the last four decades while the number of poorer Americans has risen dramatically.[35] Our FaceBook feeds remained cluttered with lists of "Top Ten Reasons Millennials Hate Your Church." Since the United Methodist Church in America has evolved into an overwhelming Caucasian (90%), older, and middle-class denomination, we have some work ahead of us as we seek to understand our communities. While John Wesley said "the world is my parish," we don't even take ownership of our own neighborhoods. How can we partner with (and expect) a new pastor to engage and impact the community if we don't keep up ourselves?

We often expect our pastor to be involved in the community, representing the church, but way too often, we forget that we can (and shall even suggest must) be ambassadors of our congregation as well. In order to adequately introduce our new pastoral leader to the community, and be full

---

34 Thompson, Derek, "Where Did All the Workers Go? 60 Years of Economic Change in 1 Graph," *The Atlantic*. January 26, 2012. http://www.theatlantic.com/business/archive/2012/01/where-did-all-the-workers-go-60-years-of-economic-change-in-1-graph/252018/).

35 Pew Research Center, "The American Middle Class Is Losing Ground." December 9, 2015. See http://www.pewsocialtrends.org/2015/12/09/the-american-middle-class-is-losing-ground/. See more excellent studies about change, demographics and culture at http://www.pewsocial-trends.org/.

partners in creating ministries that reach out beyond our walls, we must get out of our own comfort zones. One way to do that is by beginning a study of your demographics from MissionInsite or another vendor. Be intentional in naming and claiming your mission field before creating the report. Don't make the mistake of just taking the default mission field area in the program. As you look through the report, how does the report's numbers on the community match your congregation's statistics? Who is missing or underrepresented? When you plug your congregation's household data in, where are your member's homes clustered? Knowing this information before your new pastor arrives will give you all a great start on deeper conversations about your church's IMPACT and relevance in the community.

Another way to understand your community is to schedule a neighborhood prayer walk soon after the new pastor arrives, as a way to get to know both the pastor and the community. Gather the group at the church or a community spot (i.e. park or town square). Pray as a group before you depart in twos or threes asking God to reveal to each prayer God's desired future for the church by being open to seeing the mission field through the eyes of Jesus. If the prayer walkers were walking in the sandals of Jesus, what would they see, hear, feel and experience that would identify IMPACT the church is called to make. What burdens, needs, joys, concerns, is God asking the church to take responsibility for in the mission field?

Prayer walking allows us to slow down and see the community in a new way. Most of the time, we drive through the neighborhood at vehicle speeds thinking of only getting to the final destination. Prayer walking allows us to see such things as people, individual homes, businesses, community spaces with a more comprehensive understanding. We are not suggesting you knock on doors (on this first walk), but a prayer walker might stop in front of a home with an obvious need (broken down car in the yard) and offer a silent prayer.

Prayer walking is not a team sport or a social time. It is a time of holy reflection and being with God as it all relates to seeing your community with fresh eyes. After the prayer walk, gather the team back together. Ask each person individually what God revealed to her/him during the walk. Identify common themes. What did we learn? What is God's call on the future of the church as it relates to the community in reaching new people?

Experiencing a shared prayer for impacting the community for Christ is an amazing way to bond with a new pastor. Just don't limit praying and prayer walking in times of pastoral transition. Bathe all we do and all we are planning in prayer!

When we coach and consult a congregation, we often say that the members of the church are the "mission field experts." That is certainly true in that there is never a pre-packaged solution that never needs adapting to fit a particular congregation's needs. However, expertise needs *continual* work to stay current.

Instead of expecting your new pastor to "figure it out," take responsibility for understanding and connecting with your mission field and be intentional in how you interpret your church's potential IMPACT with the incoming pastor.

Strategic and Intentional Relationship Building

The days when a new pastor can arrive at any congregation that worships over 75 and simply get to know folks informally and over time are now over. The mission of the church simply can't wait for us to slowly get our act together! Worship attendance patterns are erratic nationwide. The sustainability of congregations of all sizes is perpetually in question. For many congregations, especially those trying hard to make a Christ-centered impact in their communities, the financial margin between being fully resourced for ministry and being in mission-stopping debt is incredibly tight. So, for structural and cultural reasons and for the sake of the congregation's IMPACT, new pastors are being trained to enter congregations with a plan for strategic and intentional relationship building. As leaders in the congregation, you need to assist your new pastor build relationships that are strategic to the congregation's mission, while also supporting the pastor in becoming the pastor of the larger congregation. Leaving this all up to the pastor to figure out for herself puts the very future of your congregation's IMPACT at risk. A new pastor only has a short window to make a great first impression and build trust. Your support during the transition could make the difference.

The Staff/Pastor Parish Committee or transition team should work with the incoming pastor well before she or he arrives to arrange for gatherings for the new pastor in a listening tour, cottage conversations and/or a set of town hall gatherings. Depending on the culture of the community or church, these could be at member's homes, the church parlor, or even condo or homeowners' association common rooms. Take responsibility for inviting members, hosting the event, taking notes (letting the pastor be free to engage fully in the conversation), and even driving the pastor to the events. Usually, the agenda is simple, with time for members to go around the room introducing themselves and sharing what they love about the church along with their hopes for future impact. Jim Griffith and Jim Ozier suggest handing out notecards and inviting the members to write down short answers to three questions:

- *What is one thing I need to know about the church?*
- *What is one way we are going to reach new people?*
- *What is one dream you have for the church?*

Taking one question at a time, everyone can share their answers with the group. Using the notecards helps keep folks on track and generous with one another's time. The note-cards are then taken home by note-taker and compiled, along with the meeting notes for the pastor and lay leadership.[36]

While this system may seem a bit bureaucratic to some reading this, it actually serves several excellent goals. First, it creates space for *everyone* to have an opportunity to share their journey, thoughts, and spiritual calling. In today's culture, with an array of technology platforms to share one's thoughts available at our fingertips, we ironically enough don't spend much time actually listening to each other! Second, intentional groups provide some places for the new pastor to see how members react and listen to one another's

---

36 Ozier, Jim, and Jim Griffith. *The Changeover Zone: Successful Pastoral Transitions.* Nashville: Abingdon Press, 2016, pp 69-71.

ideas. A new pastor is often cornered during the first few weeks by several members who have been waiting to share a ministry idea that multiple former pastors and the church's lay leadership have rejected because it was unworkable or strayed too far from the congregation's mission and vision. By hosting space for everyone, the lay leadership is creating a safe container for all kinds of ideas to be expressed without putting a new pastor in a potentially no-win situation. Third, if the gatherings are in member's homes or neighborhoods, it gives the pastor a chance to see where folks live, to pray God's blessings upon the hosts' homes, and to start imagining what ministry might look like in the community outside the church's walls and stained glass.

These introductory conversations can also be a great sharing time for the congregation too. Many times, our congregants spend most of their time with the same people in Sunday school classes, small groups, sitting beside them in worship or perhaps even interact with them socially. In order to get the most of the introductory conversations, intentionally mix up the groups the pastor is meeting with. In other words, don't have the pastor just meet with the Asbury Sunday school class. The Asbury Sunday school class know each other well, probably all raised their kids together, have common interests, and know one another's thoughts on the life of the church. If the groups are mixed with people who don't naturally spend time together, we add richness to the conversation by allowing our own congregants to hear thoughts from a different segment of the congregation. This intentional mixing of people will add IMPACT to the conversation for all!

As members of the church and the community, you can also provide a key role in helping your new pastor build the strategic community relationships she or he needs to lead your church in impacting your mission field. Perhaps a member is a teacher and can introduce your pastor to the local principal, or you are neighbors with the town mayor, or your pastor can meet the local sheriff or schedule a police ride-along through a church member who serves in law enforcement. Through your introductions with civic leaders and public servants, you can help your pastor learn about the community's challenges and needs. While your pastor could try to make these contacts themselves, cold calls like these are becoming very difficult. In addition to serving in the church, perhaps you also volunteer in a local ministry with the homeless or a local free health clinic. You could invite your pastor to assist you one evening, to meet the clients, and get to know those in needs in your community. How can you and your fellow church members be intentional in helping a newly arrived pastor (and each other) build strategic relationships?

When we talk with congregations about community engagement, a surprising number of churches ask about the pastor's involvement in civic clubs and community organizations. Many pastors will ask their lay leadership about congregational expectations concerning membership in the Kiwanis or Rotary club when they arrive in town, and this is the moment for the lay leadership to think strategically. How the pastor's relational time and energy best benefit the congregation's IMPACT for Christ? In many situations, the clubs and organizations may be small, so it might be more missional for congregation members who are club members not to expect their new pastor to join their club and instead agree among each other to rotate guest invitations for the pastor among the different clubs. That way, the new pastor

may be introduced to a larger slice of the community. There
are always exceptions, of course. Beyond the individual
interest of the pastor in a particular civic club's cause,
Blake worked with a senior pastor who was a member of
the largest chapter of a civic club in the state. Every week
at the Tuesday club lunch, church members brought guests
and introduced them to their beloved pastor, who accepted
their business cards and did amazing evangelistic follow
up. Along the way, members got to know the senior pastor
better and became equipped themselves to follow the pastor's
lead in being evangelists who follow-up and build Christ-centered relationships. In any case, the purpose remains the
same. How can your pastor, as a spiritual leader and unique
resource in your congregation, strategically and intentionally
build relationships and equip others to IMPACT the community for Jesus Christ? Are our expectations of our pastor
allowing them to hang out with only churched people or is
there an opportunity for meeting unchurched people, too?

Saying Goodbye and Hello

Throughout this chapter, we have focused on the strategic opportunity that comes when a congregation experiences
a pastoral transition. A transition is a time of simultaneously saying goodbye and saying hello. As laity, we need
to remember that, just as we are going through our own
emotions during a pastoral transition, the incoming and
outgoing pastors are also going through their own stressful
journeys of saying goodbye and hello. How we say goodbye to
an existing pastor says a lot about us as a congregation. It is
a gauge of our relational health because it demonstrates our
ability to manage complex emotions, and the entire transi-

tion serves as a case study of how the congregation orga-
nizes itself without pastoral leadership. To say goodbye
well, the church's leadership needs to be intentional in
providing space and time for the rituals of transition and
thanksgiving. Even in situations where the pastorate wasn't
as successful as hoped, there will be members grieving the
pastor's exit, or simply grieving over the change process
itself. So, use worship and other settings to provide an
honorable and respectful goodbye to your pastor. Allow
the congregation's members to show their appreciation for
the pastor's service. Saying goodbye poorly makes it much
harder for members to accept the incoming pastor, which
will mean that the new pastor's effectiveness and IMPACT
will be delayed. So, honor your former pastor's ministry
in ways suitable for your congregation, and along the way,
make it clear that the former pastor shouldn't be contacted
for pastoral needs or requests for funerals and weddings.

Greeting your new pastor also matters in ways deeper
than simple hospitality. How you say "hello" to your new
pastor tells her or him how intentionally you manage
complex processes, how deeply you value hospitality, and
how many people will "show up" when members are needed
to get something done. In many United Methodist conferences, all the transitioning pastors are moving out and
into parsonages on a single "moving day."[37] This doesn't
leave much time for you to make sure that the parsonage
and the pastor's office are ready for the new pastor, but
make arrangements with either pastor, cleaning services,
or teams of members to help get things ready. Please don't
assume things – *ask*. For example, some parsonage families

---

37 The "moving day" always seems to land on the hottest day of the summer. Climate scientists
should look into these phenomena.

would love help getting the moving truck unpacked, but others may have already paid for movers. Also, moving is extremely stressful and some families need a little space to "nest" before they can handle lots of guests, so don't force new pastors to choose between caring for their families or being "on duty" by greeting everyone. While we simply want to show up and care, just imagine moving to a new town, and having to deal with dozens of your new clients or patients all in your new home while also caring for a nursing newborn. So, prepare the home and office appropriately, and work out the rest with the new pastor, based on her convenience, not yours. The Lewis Center has created a list of "50 Ways to Welcome your New Pastor"[38] that offers suggestions like offering childcare during the move, cutting the grass, stocking the refrigerator with groceries, providing gift certificates to local business and restaurants, and handling all repairs before the moving van appears on the horizon. As you can tell, a proper pastoral transition not only includes your personnel committee, but also your Trustees or building maintenance committee, hospitality team, your governing board, the finance committee, and the worship planning team, along with the welcome provided by disciples in the pews. To summarize: pray for your new pastor and family, be intentional, make sure financial and facility issues are dealt with, ask questions of your new pastor so that your help is actually helpful, and offer assistance out of genuine love and hospitality, not obligation or curiosity. In other words, make your welcome about your pastor and her family,

---

38 The Lewis Center for Church Leadership provides churches and Pastor-Parish or personnel committees with a list of "50 Ways to Welcome Your New Pastor" created by Dr. Bob Crossman of PATH1 and the Arkansas Conference. Some of our suggestions can be found on his excellent short two-page checklist. See https://www.churchleadership.com/50-ways/50-ways-to-welcome-a-new-pastor/. We highly recommend sharing this list with your Pastor-Parish Committee, Trustees, and/or pastoral transition team.

not about us. How you welcome your new pastor has the potential to be a template of intentionality that you can use as you contemplate how you wish to IMPACT your larger community.

A Season for Impact: The Early "Big Win"

Long before the new pastor's moving truck is being packed, congregation leaders should already be planning for a big win. A few years ago, I (Blake) was scheduled to work with a congregation in a small Arkansas town with a population of about 3800, or 1200 households. The congregation is healthy but wanted to increase their impact in the community, so I met with their lay leadership and current pastor. My consultation was part of a follow-up to a statewide workshop based upon the book Kay authored titled *"Get Their Name: Grow Your Church by Building New Relationships."*[39] Between the times we scheduled and when I arrived in early spring, the bishop had notified the pastor and the congregation that their pastor would be moving to a new church, and the congregation's new pastor would be graduating from seminary that May. We spent some time learning about hospitality and building a faith-sharing culture, but spent most of our time sharing about what Kay calls "bridge events." Bridge events are designed to connect the community and the church to each other. Kay encourages churches to plan bridge events as a "P-Free Zone" without preaching, pressure, prayers, or pocketbooks involved. The entire event, often held off church grounds, should be designed to build relationships between members and guests, collect contact information, and do an excellent follow-up. I walked the leadership team

---

39 Farr, Bob, Douglas T. Anderson, and Kay Kotan. *Get Their Name: Grow Your Church By Building New Relationships.* Nashville: Abingdon Press, 2013.

through Kay's steps and helped them brainstorm a contextually appropriate bridge event. They decided to have a back-to-school event in mid-August and brought together teams to plan and pray for the event. By the time the new pastor arrived on July 1, all the main elements had been planned. Within a few weeks of beginning his ministry, the church hosted the Back to School Bash with hundreds attending. The congregation members intentionally used the opportunity to casually ask guests, *"Have you met our new pastor?"* creating an instant buzz in the community, and the relationships begun at the bridge event have opened up numerous avenues to have a greater impact on lives. Months after the event, the congregation was still feeling momentum from this big win, and reflecting upon what they learned about building relationships, partnering with their new pastor, and engaging their community.

Intentionality

Pastors come and go, especially in denominations with itinerant pastors. Taking ownership of our part of a clergy transition respects the incoming and outgoing pastors and respects the role of denominational leaders while also being full partners in the process. Through self-awareness and communication, we live up to our enormous responsibility as leaders and disciples in Christ's church. To be the IMPACTFUL church, we must be willing to be intentional and strategic during pastoral transitions!

Planning Your IMPACT

Questions for the Lay Leadership/Board Member

- What are the church's history and record of pastoral moves? What worked well or poorly during the last few clergy transitions?

- What will the board or S/SSPRC do to learn about the current state of the community and congregation? How will that be shared with denominational leaders, prospective pastors, and the eventual new pastor?

- How will the board or S/PPRC make communication with clergy more transparent, timely, and clear?

- What is an early "Big Win" that could help your new pastor start well and make a congregation-wide IMPACT in your community?

- How can you and fellow board members model a healthy pastoral transition for the rest of the congregation? Name one thing you can do that enables a new pastor to intentionally build strategic and IMPACTFUL relationships.

Questions for the Disciple

- How can you and your fellow church members be intentional in helping a newly arrived pastor build strategic relationships and network with the community?

- What is your plan to share your dreams, expectations, and concerns with the new pastor?

- How will you support and encourage healthy communication with the board and pastor among your fellow disciples in the pew?

- How will you encourage a culture of "Let's make an impact for Christ" during a clergy transition when most church members are taking a "Let's wait and see" approach?

Questions for the (current) Pastor & Staff

- How are your communicating with the incoming pastor and sharing critical information?

- How can you encourage and equip the congregation to set up gatherings for intentional relationship building, such as cottage meetings?

- What is the leadership and ministry style of the incoming pastor, and how will you make space in the church's systems for the new pastor's gifts?

Afterword

Rise Up and Make an IMPACT!

When you open

The United Methodist Hymnal

to page 607, you find

A Covenant Prayer in the Wesleyan Tradition.

The prayer begins,

"I am no longer my own, but thine." [40]

---

40 "A Covenant Prayer in the Wesleyan Tradition." *The United Methodist Hymnal*. Nashville, Tennessee: United Methodist Publishing House, 1989. Number 607.

The Covenant Prayer in the Wesleyan Tradition has its roots in the 18th Century Methodist movement, a movement of laity that God used to IMPACT lives, communities, and over time, the entire world. Blake actually keeps a copy of this prayer taped in the front cover of his bible, offering the prayer to God almost daily. While this book is written for us as laity, the book isn't really about "*us*." People need Christ, and the church is God's tool to employ God's people for God's work. The church as the *gathered in* and *sent out* people of God is about Jesus Christ. It is about fulfilling our mission of making disciples of Jesus Christ for the transformation of the world. The Arkansas Conference of the United Methodist church created an excellent trajectory statement that defines its purpose: *creating vital congregations that make disciples of Jesus Christ, who make disciples equipped to transform lives, communities, and the world.* What is YOUR purpose and YOUR prayer as a disciple? How often do we pray for God to bring us low, to "let me be empty," or to "put me to suffering" if that is what it takes for the Kingdom of God to be built up?

As laity and lay leaders of congregations, we do well to remember that our whole reason for gathering, for owning church property, for having ministries -- it is all tied to our disciple-making purpose, and IMPACT always starts with the transformation of individual lives. "I am no longer my own, but thine," indeed!

This 18th Century-inspired Wesleyan Covenant Prayer is filled with words of self-sacrifice, of putting the mission ahead of our own wants and desires and plans. Blake's daughter is a theater major in a performing arts high school. She and her friends have kept the album of Lin-Manuel Miranda's hit Broadway musical *Hamilton* on autoplay for a few years now. It is also inspired by the events of 18th Century -- in this case Alexander Hamilton's life in Revolutionary-War era America. The first act has a song titled, "I'm Not Throwing Away My Shot" which combines Hamilton's own desire to achieve greatness with the opportunity for the colonies to (as the chorus goes) "RISE UP" against King George of England:

We're gonna rise up! Time to take a shot![41]

It's time for us as laity to rise up out of our complacency and rise up out of our pews and rise up to make a real IMPACT in our communities. We need to be mouth-watering hungry for making and equipping disciples who can make more disciples.

IMPACT isn't about saving our church. It isn't about keeping the lights on in the sanctuary, the budget in the black, or a full-time preacher on the payroll. IMPACT is about having a God-sized dream for our church and going for it.

- Rise up and IMPACT Christ's church you are serving.

- Rise up and IMPACT culture in your community.

- Rise up and IMPACT lives through your discipleship by discipling others.

- Rise up and IMPACT relationships by investing in new people in your neighborhood.

- Rise up and IMPACT serving people in the name of Jesus demonstrating His love and grace.

- Rise up and IMPACT worship using cultural competence relevant to create a compelling experience for your neighbors.

41 Miranda, Lin-Manuel. "My Shot." *Hamilton: An American Musical.* 2015.

Rise up and IMPACT lay leadership by investing in and equipping the next generations of leaders.

Rise up and IMPACT a pastoral transition with an attitude of opportunity.

Throughout this book, we asked A LOT of questions. Your answers matter. In a way, you were our co-authors, writing the conclusion to every chapter for your corner of God's mission field. God has raised you and your church up for this moment (for such a time as this![42]) and for your community. Leadership often starts by asking better questions. Of course, the next step is taking action -- taking your shot at making an IMPACT. Where is your low-hanging fruit? Where can your IMPACT team have an early Big Win to build momentum for some much more difficult cultural changes that will be needed to reach your congregation's full potential? Our hope in this book to empower the laity to rise up and make a God-sized IMPACT in today's world, all for the glory of Jesus Christ.

Pray Constantly!

Rise up!

Take your shot at making an IMPACT in the name of Jesus!

---

42 Esther 4:14

Other books from
Market Square Books

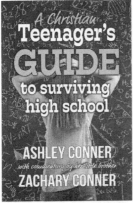

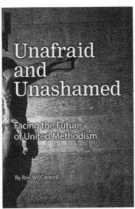

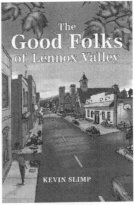

A Christian Teenager's Guide
To Surviving High School
Ashley Connor

Unafraid and Unashamed
Facing the Future of United Methodism
Wil Cantrell

The Good Folks
of Lennox Valley
Kevin Slimp

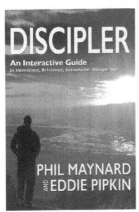

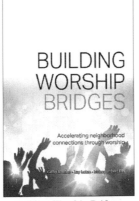

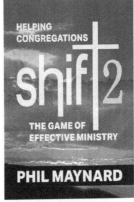

Discipler
An Interactive Guide
Phil Maynard and Eddie Pipkin

Building Worship Bridges
Cathy Townley, Kay Kotan,
and Bishop Robert Farr

Helping Congregations Shift 2
the Game of Effective Ministry
Phil Maynard

marketsquarebooks.com

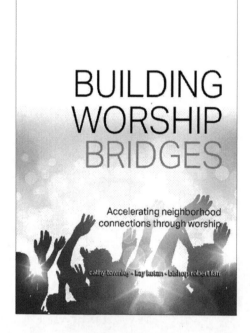

Building Worship Bridges

Cathy Townley, Kay Kotan,
and Bishop Robert Farr

Made in the USA
Middletown, DE
14 August 2019